Writing from Ca

Figures in a Landscape

Writing from Australia edited by Wendy Morgan
Writing from Canada edited by Jim Rice and Mike Hayhoe
Writing from India edited by Lakshmi Holmström and Mike Hayhoe
Writing from Ireland edited by Valerie Quinlivan
Writing from South Africa edited by Anthony Adams and Ken Durham

Figures in a Landscape

Writing from Canada

Jim Rice and Mike Hayhoe

Published by the Press Syndicate of the University of Cambridge
The Pitt Building, Trumpington Street, Cambridge CB2 1RP
40 West 20th Street, New York, NY 10011-4211, USA
10 Stamford Road, Oakleigh, Melbourne 3166, Australia

First published 1994

Printed in Great Britain at the University Press, Cambridge

A catalogue record for this book is available from the British Library

Library of Congress cataloguing in publication data
Rice. Jim.
Writing from Canada / Jim Rice and Mike Hayhoe.
p. cm. – (Figures in a landscape)
1. Canada – Literary collections. 2. Canadian literature.
I. Hayhoe. Mike. II. Title. III. Series.
PR9194.52.C3W75 1994
810.9′3271 – dc20 93–11687 CIP

ISBN 0 521 42305 8 paperback

VN

Contents

Acknowledgments

Many people in Canada and the United Kingdom have helped in the making of this book. We would like to thank the students at Queen Elizabeth High School, Halifax, Nova Scotia and at Hethersett High School, Norfolk, England who listened to, read and discussed many of the stories which appear here—and many more; our teacher colleagues in Canada and in England who have given us so much of their time and their advice in finding and selecting stories—Cate Allen (Halifax, Nova Scotia), Pat Boyle (Halifax, Nova Scotia), Alysoun Fenn (St Ives, England), Jean Hayhoe (Hethersett, England), Michael Leclerc (Montreal), Joanne Peters (Winnipeg); Susan Gibson-Garvery (Dalhousie Art Gallery) for her time, knowledge and insight in selecting images for this book; Michael Nowlan (New Brunswick) and Vivien Hughes (Canadian High Commission, United Kingdom) for their generous support; the Canadian Council of Teachers of English and Language Arts for enabling us to share the making of this book with colleagues at its national convention in Montreal.

Thanks are due to the following for permission to reproduce illustrations: p. 4 Paterson Ewen, Collection of the Carmen Lamanna Estate, Toronto; p. 14 Holman Eskimo Co-op; p. 16 and p. 24 Glenbow Collection, Calgary, Alberta, Canada, © Degen Lindner; p. 40 Survivor Wandering, etching, 1969 by David Blackwood; p. 54 Canadian Museum of Civilization, negative no. S80–1021; p. 64 Nigel Roe; p. 76 National Gallery of Canada, Ottawa; p. 88 John McKinnon, photographed by Peter MacCallum; p. 92 Marian Scott; p. 102 estate of the artist, photo by Ayriss-Reeves, Toronto; p. 114 Dalhousie Art Gallery; p. 118 Collection of the Mackenzie Art Gallery, gift of Mr. David Thauberger; p. 124 estate of the artist and the photographer, Findlay Muir; p. 132 Lawrence Paul; p. 138 Tourism British Columbia, London.

Thanks are due to the following for permission to reproduce stories: p. 3 'A Field of Wheat' by Sinclair Ross from *The Lamp at Noon* by Sinclair Ross, used by permission of the Canadian publishers, McClelland & Stewart, Toronto; p. 13 'The Custom' by Charlie Patsauq from *Paper Stays Put* by Robin Gedaloff; p. 17 'By the River' by Jack Hodgins from *Spit Delaney's Island* by Jack Hodgins © 1976 reprinted by permission of Macmillan Canada; p. 25 'The Wedding Gift' by Thomas Raddall © Thomas Raddall;

p. 39 'The Winter Dog' by Alistair MacLeod from *As Birds Bring Forth the Sun* by Alistair MacLeod, used by permission of the Canadian publishers, McClelland & Stewart, Toronto; p. 55 'An Afternoon in Bright Sunlight' by Shirley Bruised Head © Shirley Bruised Head; p. 63 'Saturday Climbing' by W.D. Valgardson from *What Can't be Changed Shouldn't be Mourned*, copyright © 1993 by W.D. Valgardson, published by Douglas & McIntyre, reprinted by permission; p. 75 'An Ounce of Cure' by Alice Munro copyright © by Alice Munro, reprinted by arrangement with Virginia Barber Literary Agency, Inc; p. 87 'The Sweeper' by Gaetan Brulotte from The Porcupine's Quill edition of *The Secret Voice*, 1982; p. 93 'Getting Bonded' by Brian Fawcett from Capital Tales © 1984 Brian Fawcett; Talon Books Ltd., Vancouver, Canada, all rights reserved; p. 101 'The Knife Sharpener' by Bonnie Burnard from *Women of Influence* by Bonnie Burnard published in Great Britain by The Women's Press Ltd., 1993, 34 Great Sutton Street, London EC1V 0DX, used by permission of The Women's Press Ltd. © 1988 by Bonnie Burnard; p.113 'Nipikti the Old Man Carver' by Alootook Ipellie from *Paper Stays Put* by Robin Gedaloff; p. 117 'Flowers for Weddings and Funerals' by Sandra Birdsell from Agassiz Stories Turnstone Press, 1987 © Sandra Birdsell, printed with permission; p. 125 'No Rinsed Blue Sky, No Red Flower Fences' by Dionne Brand © Dionne Brand; p. 133 'The Serpent's Egg' by Gilbert Oskaboose from *Our Bit of Truth: An Anthology of Canadian Native Literature*; p. 137 'Everyone Talked Loudly in Chinatown' by Anne Jew © Anne Jew.

Every attempt has been made to locate copyright holders for all material in this book. The publishers would be glad to hear from anyone whose copyright has been unwittingly infringed.

Introduction
Welcome to Canada—mine and yours

Over the last three years, Mike Hayhoe and I have read close to a thousand stories written by Canadians, trying to find tales that would be enjoyable and challenging and which would tell you something about Canada. We wanted a collection which would perhaps extend your file of images and which might challenge stereotypes about this country and its people. We also wanted to represent the many different people who call themselves Canadian so that you might see Canada not as a homogeneous mass but as a federation of communities which has been called a cultural mosaic. A brief book such as this has had to exclude hundreds of the voices which we wanted to include. How many more would have been needed to help create a true picture of Canada and its people? You and I will have to hope that the stories which appear here *suggest* much more than they state and that they will help you to imagine the greater landscape of places and people which they evoke.

The Inuit and the First Nations people (erroneously and offensively called "Red Indians") were the original inhabitants of what is now called Canada and they have felt deeply the various waves of immigration which came from across the Atlantic. You can see for yourself how many of these stories have authors with English and Scottish names. But another great European nation was involved in the early conquering of Canada—France—and French and English are the official national languages. Since the turn of the century, other people have emigrated to Canada, especially from Central Europe, with more recent immigrants coming from the Caribbean and the Far East. Canada is a nation of many peoples, many histories—many figures in a variety of landscapes which make the second largest nation on Earth.

That variety of peoples is reflected in its many languages, from the Inuktitut of the Inuit and the languages of the Blackfoot, Ojibway, Iroquois and other First Nations people to the German, Ukrainian, Icelandic, Gaelic, Cantonese, Italian and Creole and other languages that you will hear in parts of Canada. Sometimes, in reading a story in this volume you may find a word rooted in one of these languages—you may find the glossary at the back helpful on these occasions—but Canada's English language remains easily recognizable as English.

How will these stories help you to imagine Canada? In one sense, a
countries are unimaginable. Even the smallest country contains and generat
an infinite mosaic of peoples, locales, cultures, voices, attitudes, and idea
But Canada is additionally unimaginable because it is so hard to experien
directly. I am unlikely to visit in my lifetime all its provinces and territorie
nor am I likely to travel its width from Atlantic to Pacific or its depth from th
forty-ninth parallel to the North Pole.

Statistics tell me very little. What does it mean to say that Canada is 3.8
million square miles, a third bigger than Australia and three times the area
India? What does it mean to say that Canada is forty times the size of Gre
Britain, with a population of 27 million, half that of Britain? What facts an
figures would help someone living in any other country to start to gras
Canada? Would it help to know that in a prairie city such as Saskatoon th
temperature ranges from an average of 19 °C in July to *minus* 19 °C
January? What if I tell you that it would be physically impossible for o
driver to undertake a non-stop car journey across Canada, from East to Wes
because it would take eight days? In Canada, there are areas larger than th
whole of England where fewer than a hundred people live. So much
Canada remains massive and massively empty of people. Even the maj
cities are different. While the centres of some of the older cities can be said
be like the major cities of such countries as Britain, most of them show sig
of their recent development with their skyscraper centres and suburba
sprawl.

But that is not how I *imagine* Canada. Like anyone else, I have to compo
Canada from my own myriad experiences. My Canada, insofar as I am ab
to imagine it, is a collection of places, most of which I have been to, with som
that I know very well from direct experience. But there are also some tha
know from images in books and from television, and from the stories tha
have heard or read. If we were to meet, I could show you the part of Cana
where I live—the Atlantic Maritimes—but I leave Alistair MacLeod a
Thomas Raddall to tell you about its landscape and its people instead. I ha
never been to Canada's Far North, to the parts where the summer knows n
night and the winter sees no day, but these are certainly part of my imagin
Canada which I have experienced and come to know through stories about
You too will share in experiencing my Far North when you read the tales to
here by the Inuit writers Ipellie and Patsauq.

The landscapes of some of these stories will appear unfamiliar, eve foreign to you, but their people will be recognizable because they are portraits of people living in a real world—recognizable but not familiar. I think we are all in some measure shaped by the environments in which we grow up and live. We are all human and, in important ways, that makes us all alike; but we are also different, partly because we live in different cultural, psychological and geographical landscapes. The term "foreigner" reminds us that each of us bears the imprint of the place that we call home. So it is with stories. The stories we tell are influenced in subtle ways by the landscapes in which they are written—and those in which you, as a reader, experience them. In this book, you will encounter people in the huge and lonely expanses of the Prairies or the Far North; the oppressive enclosures of the great forests; the large and faceless suburbs and bustling life of Canada's few large cities. As you set these figures in the landscape of your mind, you will be creating your Canada, although there is so much more for you to know—and there are so very many more tales to tell you.

Jim Rice
Halifax, Nova Scotia

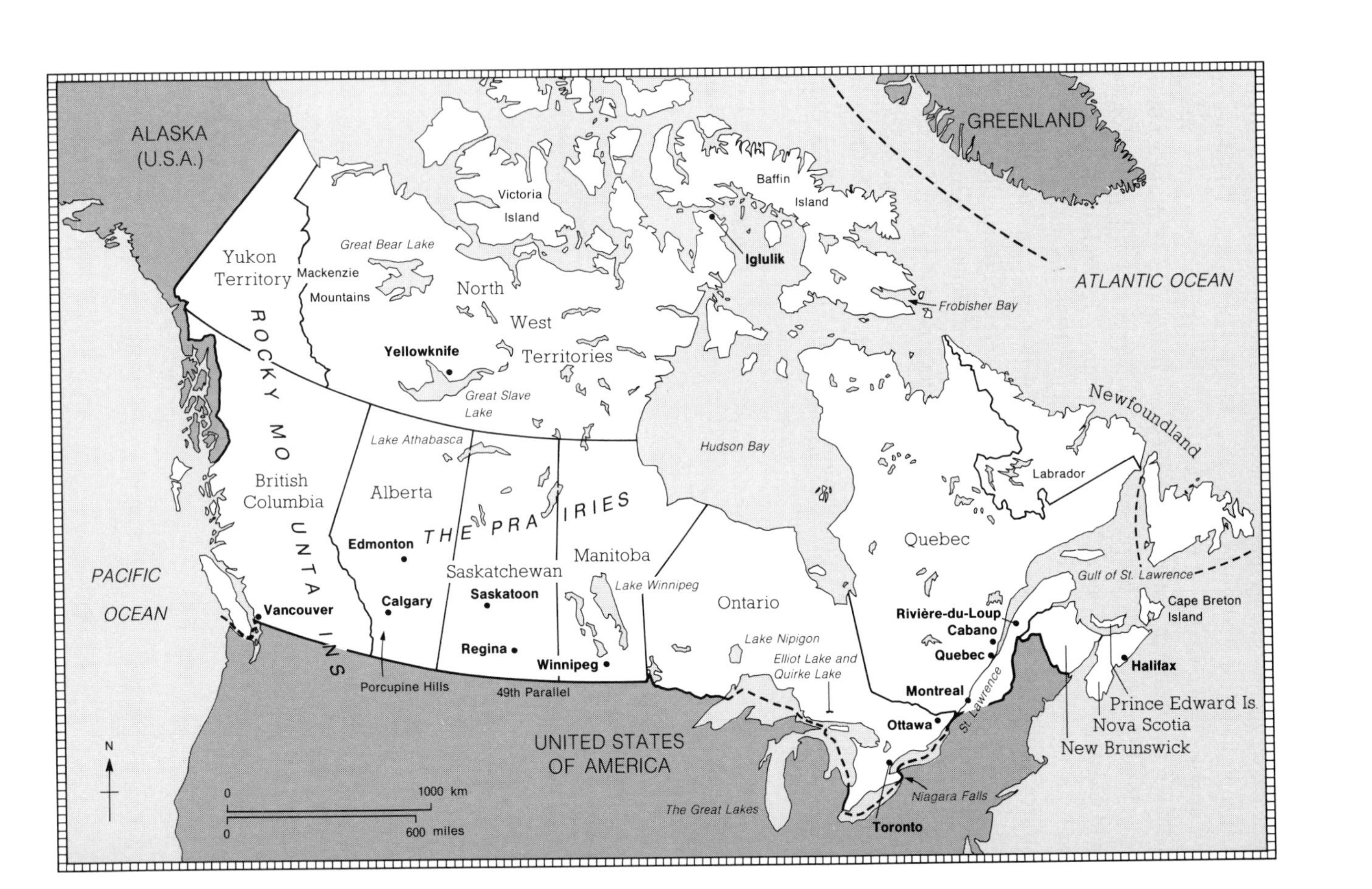
ALASKA
(U.S.A.)
GREENLAND
Baffin
Island
Victoria
Island
Iglulik
Yukon
Territory
Mackenzie
Mountains
Great Bear Lake
North
West
Territories
ATLANTIC OCEAN
Frobisher Bay
Yellowknife
Great Slave
Lake
ROCKY MOUNTAINS
Newfoundland
Hudson Bay
Lake Athabasca
Labrador
British
Columbia
Alberta
THE PRAIRIES
Quebec
Edmonton
Manitoba
Saskatchewan
Gulf of St. Lawrence
PACIFIC
OCEAN
Lake Winnipeg
Ontario
Calgary
Saskatoon
Cape Breton
Island
Vancouver
Rivière-du-Loup
Cabano
Lake Nipigon
Regina
Quebec
Winnipeg
Elliot Lake and
Quirke Lake
Halifax
Porcupine Hills
49th Parallel
Montreal
St. Lawrence
Prince Edward Is.
Ottawa
Nova Scotia
UNITED STATES
OF AMERICA
New Brunswick
N
0
1000 km
0
600 miles
Niagara Falls
The Great Lakes
Toronto

The Great Landscape

A Field of Wheat

SINCLAIR ROSS 1968

From the centre of Canada the Great Plains stretch westward to the Rocky Mountains. Once these were the Prairies, the hunting grounds of the First Nations people; now, they are the great wheatlands, tamed by massive ploughs and harvesters. But the weather cannot be tamed, whether it be the incessant scorching winds which brought about the Great Drought of the early 1930s or, as here, a sudden moment of winter violence in the middle of summer. In such a harsh and unpredictable world, survival demands extremes of courage, compassion and endurance.

It was the best crop of wheat that John had ever grown; sturdy, higher than the knee, the heads long and filling well; a still, heat-hushed mile of it, undulating into a shimmer of summer-colts and crushed horizon blue. Martha finished pulling the little patch of mustard that John had told her about at noon, stood a minute with her shoulders strained back to ease the muscles that were sore from bending, then bunched up her apron filled with the yellow-blossomed weeds and started towards the road. She walked carefully, placing her feet edgeways between the rows of wheat to avoid trampling and crushing the stalks. The road was only a few rods distant, but several times she stopped before reaching it, holding her apron with one hand close against her skirts, luxuriant and tall. Once she looked back, her eyes shaded, across the wheat to the dark fallow land beside it. John was there; she could see the long, slow-settling plume of dust thrown up by the horses and the harrow-cart. He was a fool for work, John. This year he was farming the whole section of land without help, managing with two outfits of horses, one for the morning and one for the afternoon; six, and sometimes even seven hours a shift.

It was John who gave such allure to the wheat. She thought of him hunched black and sweaty on the harrow-cart, twelve hours a day, smothering in dust, shoulders sagged wearily beneath the glare of the sun. Her fingers touched the stalks of grain again and tightened on a supple blade until they made it squeak like a mouse. A crop like this was coming to him. He had had his share of failures and setbacks, if ever a man had, twenty times over.

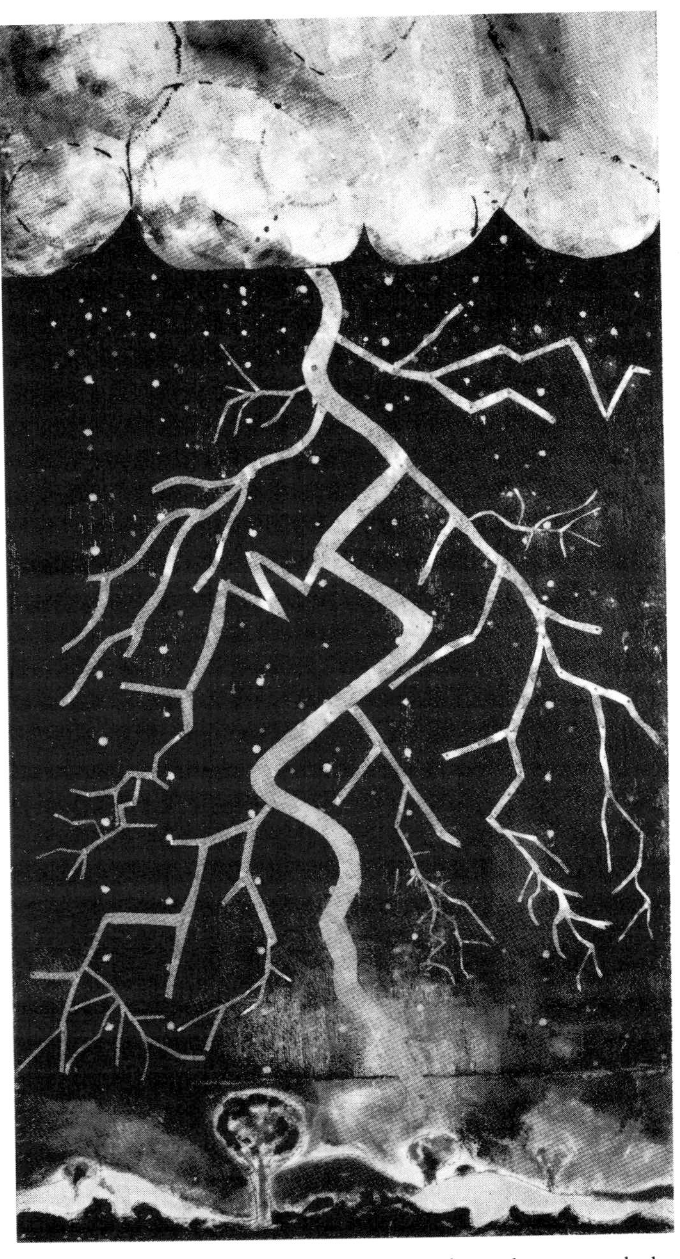

Forked Lighting by Paterson Ewen, 1971, acrylic and metal on gouged plywood.

Martha was thirty-seven. She had clinched with the body and substance of life; had loved, borne children —a boy had died—and yet the quickest aches of life, travail, heartbrokenness, they had never wrung as the wheat wrung. For the wheat allowed no respite. Wasting and unending it was struggle, struggle against wind and insects, drought and weeds. Not an heroic struggle to give a man courage and resolve, but a frantic, unavailing one. They were only poor, taunted, driven things; it was the wheat that was invincible. They only dreaded, built bright futures; waited for the first glint of green, watched timorous and eager while it thickened, merged, and at last leaned bravely to a ripple in the wind; then followed every slip of cloud into the horizon, turned to the wheat and away again. And it died tantalizingly sometimes, slowly: there would be a cool day, a pittance of rain.

Or perhaps it lived, perhaps the rain came, June, July, even into August, hope climbing, wish-patterns painted on the future. And then one day a clench and tremble to John's hand; his voice faltering, dull. Grasshoppers perhaps, sawflies or rust; no matter, they would grovel for a while, stand back helpless, then go on again. Go on in bitterness and cowardice, because there was nothing else but going-on.

She had loved John, for these sixteen years had stood close watching while he died—slowly, tantalizingly, as the parched wheat died. He had grown unkempt, ugly, morose. His voice was gruff, contentious, never broke into the deep, strong laughter that used to make her feel she was living at the heart of things. John was gone, love was gone; there was only wheat.

She plucked a blade; her eyes travelled hungrily up and down the field. Serene now, all its sting and torment sheathed. Beautiful, more beautiful than Annabelle's poppies, than her sunsets. Theirs—all of it. Three hundred acres ready to give perhaps a little of what it had taken from her—John, his love, his lips unclenched.

Three hundred acres. Bushels, thousands of bushels, she wouldn't even try to think how many. And prices up this year. It would make him young again, lift his head, give him spirit. Maybe he would shave twice a week as he used to when they were first married, buy new clothes, believe in himself again.

She walked down the road towards the house, her steps quickening to the pace of her thoughts until the sweat clung to her face like little beads of oil. It was the children now, Joe and Annabelle: this winter perhaps they could send them to school in town and let them take music lessons. Annabelle, anyway. At a pinch Joe could wait a while; he was only eight. It wouldn't take

Annabelle long to pick up her notes; already she played hymn tunes by ear on the organ. She was bright, a real little lady for manners; among town people she would learn a lot. The farm was no place to bring her up. Running wild and barefoot, what would she be like in a few years? Who would ever want to marry her but some stupid country lout?

John had never been to school himself; he knew what it meant to go through life with nothing but his muscles to depend upon; and that was it dread that Annabelle and Joe would be handicapped as he was, that was what had darkened him, made him harsh and dour. That was why he breasted the sun and dust a frantic, dogged fool, to spare them, to help them to a life that offered more than sweat and debts. Martha knew. He was a slow, inarticulate man, but she knew. Sometimes it even vexed her, brought a wrinkle of jealousy, his anxiety about the children, his sense of responsibility where they were concerned. He never seemed to feel that he owed her anything, never worried about her future. She could sweat, grow flat-footed and shapeless but that never bothered him.

Her thoughts were on their old, trudging way, the way they always went but then she halted suddenly, and with her eyes across the wheat again found freshening promise in its quiet expanse. The children must come first, but sh and John—mightn't there be a little of life left for them too? A man wa young at thirty-nine. And if she didn't have to work so hard, if she could ge some new clothes, maybe some of the creams and things that other women had . . .

As she passed through the gate, Annabelle raced across the yard to mee her. "Do you know what Joe's done? He's taken off all his clothes and he's in the trough with Nipper!" She was a lanky girl, sunburned, barefoot, her fac oval and regular, but spoiled by an expression that strained her mouth and brows into a reproachful primness. It was Martha who had taught her th expression, dinning manners and politeness into her, trying to make he better than the other little girls who went to the country school. She went on her eyes wide and aghast, "And when I told him to come out he stood righ up, all bare, and I had to come away."

"Well, you tell him he'd better be out before I get there."

"But how can I tell him? He's all bare."

Then Joe ran up, nothing on but little cotton knee-pants, strings of gree scum from the water-trough still sticking to his face and arms. "She's bee peekin'." He pointed at Annabelle. "Nipper and me just got into the troug to get cooled off, and she wouldn't mind her own business."

"Don't you tell lies about me." Annabelle pounced on him and slapped his bare back. "You're just a dirty little pig anyway, and the horses don't want to drink after you've been in the trough."

Joe squealed, and excited by the scuffle Nipper yelped and spattered Martha with a spray of water from his coat and tail. She reached out to cuff him, missed, and then to satisfy the itch in her fingers seized Joe and boxed his ears. "You put your shirt on and then go and pick peas for supper. Hurry now, both of you, and only the fat ones, mind. No, not you, Annabelle." There was something about Annabelle's face, burned and countrified, that changed Martha's mind. "You shell the peas when he gets them. You're in the sun too much as it is."

"But I've got a poppy out and if he goes to the garden by himself he'll pick it—just for spite." Annabelle spun round, and leaving the perplexity in her voice behind her, bolted for the garden. The next minute, before Martha had even reached the house, she was back again triumphant, a big fringed pink and purple poppy in her hand. Sitting down on the doorstep to admire the gaudy petals, she complained to herself, "They go so fast—the first little winds blow them all away." On her face, lengthening it, was bitten deeply the enigma of the flowers and the naked seed-pods. Why did the beauty flash and the bony stalks remain?

Martha had clothes to iron, and biscuits to bake for supper; Annabelle and Joe quarrelled about the peas until she shelled them herself. It was hot—heat so intense and breathless that it weighed like a solid. An ominous darkness came with it, gradual and unnoticed. All at once she turned away from the stove and stood strained, inert. The silence seemed to gather itself, hold its breath. She tried to speak to Nipper and the children, all three sprawled in a heap alongside the house, but the hush over everything was like a raised finger, forbidding her.

A long immobile minute; suddenly a bewildering awareness that the light was choked; and then, muffled, still distant, but charged with resolution, climaxing the stillness, a slow, long brooding heave of thunder.

Martha darted to the door, stumbled down the step and around the corner of the house. To the west there was no sky, only a gulf of blackness, so black that the landscape seemed slipping down the neck of a funnel. Above, almost overhead, a heavy, hard-lined bank of cloud swept its way across the sun-white blue in august, impassive fury.

"Annabelle!" She wanted to scream a warning, but it was a bare whisper. In front of her the blackness split—an abrupt, unforked gash of light as if angry hands had snatched to seal the rent.

"Annabelle! Quick—inside—!" Deep in the funnel, shaggy thunder rolled, emerged and shook itself, then with hurtling strides leaped up to drum and burst itself on the advancing peak of cloud.

"Joe, come back here!" He was off in pursuit of Nipper, who had broken away from Annabelle when she tried to pull him into the house. "Before I warm you!"

Her voice broke. She stared into the blackness. There it was—the hail again—the same white twisting little cloud against the black one—just as she had seen it four years ago.

She craned her neck, looking to see whether John was coming. The wheat, the acres and acres of it, green and tall, if only he had put some insurance on it. Damned mule—just work and work. No head himself and too stubborn to listen to anyone else.

There was a swift gust of wind, thunder in a splintering avalanche, the ragged hail-cloud low and close. She wheeled, with a push sent Annabelle toppling into the house, and then ran to the stable to throw open the big doors. John would turn the horses loose—surely he would. She put a brace against one of the doors, and bashed the end into the ground with her foot. Surely—but he was a fool—such a fool at times. It would be just like him to risk a runaway for the sake of getting to the end of the field.

The first big drops of rain were spitting at her before she reached the house. Quietly, breathing hard, she closed the door, numb for a minute, afraid to think or move. At the other side of the kitchen Annabelle was tussling with Joe, trying to make him go down cellar with her. Frightened a little by her mother's excitement, but not really able to grasp the imminence of danger, she was set on exploiting the event; and to be compelled to seize her little brother and carry him down cellar struck her imagination as a superb way of crystallizing for all time the dreadfulness of the storm and her own dramatic part in it. But Martha shouted at her hoarsely, "Go and get pillows. Here, Joe, quick, up on the table." She snatched him off his feet and set him on the table beside the window. "Be ready now when the hail starts, to hold the pillow tight against the glass. You, Annabelle, stay upstairs at the west window in my room."

The horses were coming, all six at a break-neck gallop, terrified by the thunder and the whip stripes John had given them when he turned them loose. They swept past the house, shaking the earth, their harness jangling tinny against the brattle of thunder, and collided headlong at the stable door.

John, too; through Joe's legs Martha caught sight of his long, scarecrow shape stooped low before the rain. Distractedly, without purpose, she ran upstairs two steps at a time to Annabelle. "Don't be scared, here comes your father!" Her own voice shook, craven. "Why don't you rest your arms? It hasn't started yet."

As she spoke there was a sharp, crunching blow on the roof, its sound abruptly dead, sickening, like a weapon that has sunk deep into flesh. Wildly she shook her hands, motioning Annabelle back to the window, and started for the stairs. Again the blow came; then swiftly a stuttered dozen of them.

She reached the kitchen just as John burst in. With their eyes screwed up against the pommelling roar of the hail they stared at each other. They were deafened, pinioned, crushed. His face was a livid blank, one cheek smeared with blood where a jagged stone had struck him. Taut with fear, her throat aching, she turned away and looked through Joe's legs again. It was like a furious fountain, the stones bouncing high and clashing with those behind them. They had buried the earth, blotted out the horizon; there was nothing but their crazy spew of whiteness. She cowered away, put her hands to her ears.

Then the window broke, and Joe and the pillow tumbled off the table before the howling inrush of the storm. The stones clattered on the floor and bounded up to the ceiling, lit on the stove and threw out sizzling steam. The wind whisked pots and kettles off their hooks, tugged at and whirled the sodden curtains, crashed down a shelf of lamps and crockery. John pushed Martha and Joe into the next room and shut the door. There they found Annabelle huddled at the foot of the stairs, round-eyed, biting her nails in terror. The window she had been holding was broken too; and she had run away without closing the bedroom door, leaving a wild tide of wind upstairs to rage unchecked. It was rocking the whole house, straining at the walls. Martha ran up to close the door, and came down whimpering.

There was hail heaped on the bed, the pictures were blown off the walls and broken, the floor was swimming; the water would soak through and spoil all the ceilings.

John's face quietened her. They all crowded together, silent, averting their eyes from one another. Martha wanted to cry again, but dared not. Joe, awed to calmness, kept looking furtively at the trickle of blood on his father's face. Annabelle's eyes went wide and glassy as suddenly she began to wonder about Nipper. In the excitement and terror of the storm they had all forgotten him.

When at last they could go outside they stumbled over his body on the step. He had run away from Joe before the storm started, crawled back to the house when he saw John go in, and crouching down against the door had been beaten lifeless. Martha held back the children, while John picked up the mangled heap and hurried away with it to the stable.

Neither Joe nor Annabelle cried. It was too annihilating, too much like a blow. They clung tightly to Martha's skirts, staring across the flayed yard and garden. The sun came out, sharp and brilliant on the drifts of hail. There was an icy wind that made them shiver in their thin cotton clothes. "No, it's too cold on your feet." Martha motioned them back to the step as she started towards the gate to join John. "I want to go with your father to look at the wheat. There's nothing anyway to see."

Nothing but the glitter of sun on hailstones. Nothing but their wheat crushed into little rags of muddy slime. Here and there an isolated straw standing bolt upright in headless defiance. Martha and John walked to the far end of the field. There was no sound but their shoes slipping and rattling on the pebbles of ice. Both of them wanted to speak, to break the atmosphere of calamity that hung over them, but the words they could find were too small for the sparkling serenity of wasted field. Even as waste it was indomitable. It tethered them to itself, so that they could not feel or comprehend. It had come and gone, that was all; before its tremendousness and havoc they were prostrate. They had not yet risen to cry out or protest.

It was when they were nearly back to the house that Martha started to whimper. "I can't go on any longer; I can't, John. There's no use, we've tried." With one hand she clutched him and with the other held her apron to her mouth. "It's driving me out of my mind. I'm so tired—heart-sick of it all. Can't you see?"

He laid his big hands on her shoulders. They looked at each other for a few seconds, then she dropped her head weakly against his greasy smock. Presently he roused her. "Here come Joe and Annabelle!" The pressure of his hands tightened. His bristly cheek touched her hair and forehead. "Straighten up, quick, before they see you!"

It was more of him than she had had for years. "Yes, John, I know—I'm all right now." There was a wistful little pull in her voice as if she would have had him hold her there, but hurriedly instead she began to dry her eyes with her apron. "And tell Joe you'll get him another dog."

Then he left her and she went back to the house. Mounting within her was a resolve, a bravery. It was the warming sunlight, the strength and nearness of John, a feeling of mattering, belonging. Swung far upwards by the rush and swell of recaptured life, she was suddenly as far above the desolation of the storm as a little while ago she had been abject before it. But in the house she was alone; there was no sunlight, only a cold wind through the broken window; and she crumpled again.

She tried to face the kitchen, to get the floor dried and the broken lamps swept up. But it was not the kitchen; it was tomorrow, next week, next year. The going on, the waste of life, the hopelessness.

Her hands fought the broom a moment, twisting the handle as if trying to unscrew the rusted cap of a jar; then abruptly she let it fall and strode outside. All very fine for John: he'd talk about education for Joe and Annabelle, and she could worry where the clothes were to come from so that they could go clean and decent even to the country school. It made no difference that she had wanted to take out hail insurance. He was the one that looked after things. She was just his wife; it wasn't for her to open her mouth. He'd pat her shoulder and let her come back to this. They'd be brave, go on again, forget about the crop. Go on, go on—next year and the next—go on till they were both ready for the scrap-heap. But she'd had enough. This time he'd go on alone.

Not that she meant it. Not that she failed to understand what John was going through. It was just rebellion. Rebellion because their wheat was beaten to the ground, because there was this brutal, callous finish to everything she had planned, because she had will and needs and flesh, because she was alive. Rebellion, not John at all—but how rebel against a summer storm, how find the throat of a cloud?

So at a jerky little run she set off for the stable, for John. Just that she might release and spend herself, no matter against whom or what, unloose the fury that clawed within her, strike back a blow for the one that had flattened her.

The stable was quiet, only the push of hay as the horses nosed through the mangers, the lazy rub of their flanks and hips against the stall partitions; and before its quietness her anger subsided, took time for breath. She advanced slowly, almost on tiptoe, peering past the horses' rumps for a glimpse of John.

To the last stall, back again. And then there was a sound different from the stable sounds. She paused.

She had not seen him the first time she passed because he was pressed against one of the horses, his head pushed into the big deep hollow of its neck and shoulder, one hand hooked by the fingers in the mane, his own shoulders drawn up and shaking. She stared, thrust out her head incredulously, moved her lips, but stood silent. John sobbing there, against the horse. It was the strangest, most frightening moment of her life. He had always been so strong and grim; had just kept on as if he couldn't feel, as if there were a bull's hide over him, and now he was beaten.

She crept away. It would be unbearable to watch his humiliation if he looked up and saw her. Joe was wandering about the yard, thinking about Nipper and disconsolately sucking hailstones, but she fled past him, head down, stricken with guilty shame as if it were she who had been caught broken and afraid. He had always been so strong, a brute at times in his strength, and now—

Now—why now that it had come to this, he might never be able to get a grip of himself again. He might not want to keep on working, not if he were really beaten. If he lost heart, if he didn't care about Joe and Annabelle any more. Weeds and pests, drought and hail—it took so much fight for a man to hold his own against them all, just to hold his own, let alone make headway.

"Look at the sky!" It was Annabelle again, breathless and ecstatic. "The far one—look how it's opened like a fan!"

Withdrawn now in the eastern sky the storm clouds towered, gold-capped and flushed in the late sunlight, high, still pyramids of snowiness and shadow. And one that Annabelle pointed to apart, the farthest away of them all, this one in bronzed slow splendour spread up mountains high to a vast, plateau-like summit.

Martha hurried inside. She started the fire again, then nailed a blanket over the broken window and lit the big brass parlour lamp—the only one the storm had spared. Her hands were quick and tense. John would need a good supper tonight. The biscuits were water-soaked, but she still had the peas. He liked peas. Lucky that they had picked them when they did. This winter they wouldn't have so much as an onion or potato.

The Custom

CHARLIE PATSAUQ 1974

Inuit life in the Far North of Canada has undergone many changes but it has always involved a struggle for survival, even with the aid of such modern technology as aeroplanes, motorized sledges and rifles. In this simple and bleak tale, an Inuit high school student writes about life before such Western technology was available and of the awful, loving price which sometimes had to be paid if the people were to survive.

The old man was becoming useless to his sons. He was now becoming a burden to them. Just an old man, another mouth to feed. Useless weight when he sat on the sled as the dogs pulled. The village was slowly starving, this was the time of famine for the Eskimos. The hunters were now deciding where to go. The old man knew it was up to his sons whether or not he was to be left behind. He knew there were many reasons for him to be abandoned when the village moved as was the custom when old people became useless. Recently when other people began to talk of moving to other hunting grounds, his sons became less talkative, the old man knew what they were thinking about, abandon or take him?

The day came to move. There were few dogs, the majority of the dogs had died of starvation. The dead dogs had been fed to the other dogs to keep them alive. The people, too, had eaten the dead dogs in desperation. It was time to move. The sons loaded their sled with only the essentials. Then they came inside the igloo and sat beside the old man.

The older son spoke first, "Father, we love and respect you very much but we will have to leave you behind. We would unhesitatingly stay here and die with you but the people need us. Many hunters have died during this great hunger, so the people need as many hunters as possible. Please understand, father."

"I understand, I have been anticipating this. Leave me behind, leave with my blessings," said the old man.

"Father," said the older son, "how do you want to die? Do you want us to hang you, or do you want to die by my harpoon or should we just leave you behind to starve to death?"

Calling for Seals by Helen Kalvak (printer, Louis Nigiyok), stonecut.

"Hang me, my dear sons, I command you to do it."

The sons slowly went up and put a hole in the top of the igloo and put a sealskin rope through it. They formed a noose and put it on the old man's neck after they had let him stand on a snow block a foot high from the ground. Neither of the sons could bring themselves to kick the block away. Then the younger son brought up his courage. "I will kick the block away," he said to his father and brother. His brother left the igloo and went outside.

The son said to his father, "Forgive me, father, but I must do it."

"There is nothing to forgive, my son, it is the way of our people."

The younger son started crying but he kicked the block from under the old man's feet. His father did not struggle. The young son was now on his knees crying openly. His elder brother walked in with the rest of the people who had anticipated the whole thing. The people understood why they had done it and they comforted the brothers. Then they went to their dogs and started moving out, with the brothers leading, both brothers weeping with grief.

Forest by Ernest Lindner, 1940, linocut on paper.

By the River

JACK HODGINS 1976

Canada is the second biggest nation in the world. There was a time when many people sought their future in its vast wilderness of plains, lakes and forests but nowadays people are moving back towards the great cities and the land grows emptier. And yet, as this sad and compassionate tale shows, some individuals cling to dreams of love and loyalty and of living a simpler life, whatever the reality may be.

But listen, she thinks, it's nearly time.

And flutters, leaf-like, at the thought. The train will rumble down the valley, stop at the little shack to discharge Styan, and move on. This will happen in half an hour and she has a mile still to walk.

Crystal Styan walking through the woods, through bush, is not pretty. She knows that she is not even a little pretty, though her face is small enough, and pale, and her eyes are not too narrow. She wears a yellow wool sweater and a long cotton skirt and boots. Her hair, tied back so the branches will not catch in it, hangs straight and almost colourless down her back. Some day, she expects, there will be a baby to play with her hair and hide in it like someone behind a waterfall.

She has left the log cabin, which sits on the edge of the river in a stand of birch, and now she follows the river bank upstream. A mile ahead, far around the bend out of sight, the railroad tracks pass along the rim of their land and a small station is built there just for them, for her and Jim Styan. It is their only way in to town, which is ten miles away and not much of a town anyway when you get there. A few stores, a tilted old hotel, a movie theatre.

Likely, Styan would have been to a movie last night. He would have stayed the night in the hotel, but first (after he had seen the lawyer and bought the few things she'd asked him for) he would pay his money and sit in the back row of the theatre and laugh loudly all the way through the movie. He always laughs at everything, even if it isn't funny, because those figures on the screen make him think of people he has known; and the thought of them exposed like this for just anyone to see embarrasses him a little and makes him want to create a lot of noise so people will know he isn't a bit like that himself.

She smiles. The first time they went to a movie together she slouched as far down in the seat as she could so no one could see she was there or had anything to do with Jim Styan.

The river flows past her almost silently. It has moved only a hundred miles from its source and has another thousand miles to go before it reaches the ocean, but already it is wide enough and fast. Right here she has more than once seen a moose wade out and then swim across to the other side and disappear into the cedar swamps. She knows something, has heard some where that farther downstream, miles and miles behind her, an Indian band once thought this river a hungry monster that liked to gobble up their people. They say that Coyote their god-hero dived in and subdued the monster and made it promise never to swallow people again. She once thought she'd like to study that kind of thing at a university or somewhere, if Jim Styan hadn't told her grade ten was good enough for anyone and a life on the road was more exciting.

What road? she wonders. There isn't a road within ten miles. They sold th rickety old blue pickup the same day they moved onto this place. The railroa was going to be all they'd need. There wasn't any place they cared to go tha the train, even this old-fashioned milk-run outfit, couldn't take them easil and cheaply enough.

But listen, she thinks, it's nearly time.

The trail she is following swings inland to climb a small bluff and for while she is engulfed by trees. Cedar and fir are dark and thick and damp. Th green new growth on the scrub bushes has nearly filled in the narrow trail. Sh holds her skirt up a little so it won't be caught or ripped, then runs and nearl slides down the hill again to the river's bank. She can see in every direction fo miles and there isn't a thing in sight which has anything to do with man

"Who needs them?" Styan said, long ago.

It was with that kind of question—questions that implied an answer s obvious only a fool would think to doubt—that he talked her first out of th classroom and then right off the island of her birth and finally up here into th mountains with the river and the moose and the railroad. It was as if he ha transported her in his falling-apart pickup not only across the province abo as far as it was possible to go, but also backwards in time, perhaps as far her grandmother's youth or even farther. She washes their coarse clothing the river and depends on the whims of the seasons for her food.

"Look!" he shouted when they stood first in the clearing above the cabi

"It's as if we're the very first ones. You and me."

They swam in the cold river that day and even then she thought of Coyote and the monster, but he took her inside the cabin and they made love on the fir-bough bed that was to be theirs for the next five years. "We don't need any of them," he sang. He flopped over on his back and shouted up into the rafters. "We'll farm it! We'll make it go. We'll make our own world!" Naked, he was as thin and pale as a celery stalk.

When they moved in he let his moustache grow long and droopy like someone in an old, brown photograph. He wore overalls which were far too big for him and started walking around as if there were a movie camera somewhere in the trees and he was being paid to act like a hillbilly instead of the city-bred boy he really was. He stuck a limp felt hat on the top of his head like someone's uncle Hiram and bought chickens.

"It's a start," he said.

"Six chickens?" She counted again to be sure. "We don't even have a shed for them."

He stood with his feet wide apart and looked at her as if she were stupid. "They'll lay their eggs in the grass."

"That should be fun," she said. "A hundred and sixty acres is a good-size pen."

"It's a start. Next spring we'll buy a cow. Who needs more?"

Yes who? They survived their first winter here, though the chickens weren't so lucky. The hens got lice and started pecking at each other. By the time Styan got around to riding in to town for something to kill the lice a few had pecked right through the skin and exposed the innards. When he came back from town they had all frozen to death in the yard.

At home, back on her father's farm in the blue mountains of the island, nothing had ever frozen to death. Her father had cared for things. She had never seen anything go so wrong there, or anyone have to suffer.

She walks carefully now, for the trail is on the very edge of the river bank and is spongy and broken away in places. The water, clear and shallow here, back-eddies into little bays where cattail and bracken grow and where water-skeeters walk on their own reflection. A beer bottle glitters where someone, perhaps a guide on the river, has thrown it—wedged between stones as if it has been there as long as they have. She keeps her face turned to the river, away from the acres and acres of forest which are theirs.

Listen, it's nearly time, she thinks. And knows that soon, from far up the

river valley, she will be able to hear the throbbing of the train, coming near.
She imagines his face at the window. He is the only passenger in the coach and sits backwards, watching the land slip by, grinning in expectation o memory or both. He tells a joke to old Bill Cobb the conductor but even in hi laughter does not turn his eyes from outside the train. One spot on hi forehead is white where it presses against the glass. His fingers run over an over the long drooping ends of his moustache. He is wearing his hat.

Hurry, hurry, she thinks. To the train, to her feet, to him.

She wants to tell him about the skunk she spotted yesterday. She wants t tell him about the stove, which smokes too much and needs some kind o clean-out. She wants to tell him about her dream; how she dreamed he wa trying to go into the river and how she pulled and hauled on his feet but h wouldn't come out. He will laugh and laugh at her when she tells him, and hi laughter will make it all right and not so frightening, so that maybe she will b able to laugh at it too.

She has rounded the curve in the river and glances back, way back, at th cabin. It is dark and solid, not far from the bank. Behind the poplars th cleared fields are yellowing with the coming of fall but now in all that pla there isn't a thing alive, unless she wants to count trees and insects. N people. No animals. It is scarcely different from her very first look at it. In fi years their dream of livestock has been shelved again and again.

Once there was a cow. A sway-backed old Jersey.

"This time I've done it right," he said. "Just look at this prize."

And stepped down off the train to show off his cow, a wide-eyed beau that looked at her through a window of the passenger coach.

"Maybe so, but you'll need a miracle, too, to get that thing down out there."

A minor detail to him, who scooped her up and swung her around a kissed her hard, all in front of the old conductor and the engineer who did even bother to turn away. "Farmers at last!" he shouted. "You can't have farm without a cow. You can't have a baby without a cow."

She put her head inside the coach, looked square into the big brown ey glanced at the sawed-off horns. "Found you somewhere, I guess," she said the cow. "Turned out of someone's herd for being too old or senile or dri up."

"An auction sale," he said, and slapped one hand on the window glass. was the only one there who was desperate. But I punched her bag and pull her tits; she'll do. There may even be a calf or two left in her sway-backed old soul."

"Come on, bossy," she said. "This is no place for you."

But the cow had other ideas. It backed into a corner of the coach and shook its lowered head. Its eyes, steady and dull, never left Crystal Styan.

"You're home," Styan said. "Sorry there's no crowd here or a band playing music, but step down anyway and let's get started."

"She's not impressed," she said. "She don't see any barn waiting out there either, not to mention hay or feed of any kind. She's smart enough to know a train coach is at least a roof over her head."

The four of them climbed over the seats to get behind her and pushed her all the way down the aisle. Then, when they had shoved her down the steps, she fell on her knees on the gravel and let out a long unhappy bellow. She looked around, bellowed again, then stood up and high-tailed it down the tracks. Before Styan even thought to go after her she swung right and headed into bush.

Styan disappeared into the bush, too, hollering, and after a while the train moved on to keep its schedule. She went back down the trail and waited in the cabin until nearly dark. When she went outside again she found him on the river bank, his feet in the water, his head resting against a birch trunk.

"What the hell," he said, and shook his head and didn't look at her.

"Maybe she'll come back," she said.

"A bear'll get her before then, or a cougar. There's no hope of that."

She put a hand on his shoulder but he shook it off. He'd dragged her from place to place right up this river from its mouth, looking and looking for his dream, never satisfied until he saw this piece of land. For that dream and for him she had suffered.

She smiles, though, at the memory. Because even then he was able to bounce back, resume the dream, start building new plans. She smiles, too, because she knows there will be a surprise today; there has always been a surprise. When it wasn't a cow it was a bouquet of flowers or something else. She goes through a long list in her mind of what it may be, but knows it will be none of them. Not once in her life has anything been exactly the way she imagined it. Just so much as foreseeing something was a guarantee it wouldn't happen, at least not in the exact same way.

"Hey you, Styan!" she suddenly calls out. "Hey you, Jim Styan. Where are you?" And laughs, because the noise she makes can't possibly make any difference to the world, except for a few wild animals that might be alarmed.

She laughs again, and slaps one hand against her thigh, and shakes her head. Just give her—how many minutes now?—and she won't be alone. These woods will shudder with his laughter, his shouting, his joy. That train, that kinky little train will drop her husband off and then pass on like a stay-stitch thread pulled from a seam.

"Hey you, Styan! What you brought this time? A gold brooch? An old nanny goat?"

The river runs past silently and she imagines that it is only shoulders she is seeing, that monster heads have ducked down to glide by but are watching her from eyes as grey as stone. She wants to scream out "Hide, you crummy cheat, my Coyote's coming home!" but is afraid to tempt even something that she does not believe in. And anyway she senses—far off—the beat of the little train coming down the valley from the town.

And when it comes into sight she is there, on the platform in front of the little sagging shed, watching. She stands tilted far out over the tracks to see, but never dares—even when it is so far away—to step down onto the ties for a better look.

The boards beneath her feet are rotting and broken. Long stems of grass have grown up through the cracks and brush against her legs. A squirrel runs down the slope of the shed's roof and yatters at her until she turns and lifts her hand to frighten it into silence.

She talks to herself, sings almost to the engine's beat—"Here he comes, here he comes"—and has her smile already as wide as it can be. She smiles into the side of the locomotive sliding past and the freight car sliding past and keeps on smiling even after the coach has stopped in front of her and it is obvious that Jim Styan is not on board.

Unless of course he is hiding under one of the seats, ready to leap up, one more surprise.

But old Bill Cobb the conductor backs down the steps, dragging a gunny sack out after him. "H'lo there, Crystal," he says. "He ain't aboard today either, I'm afraid." He works the gunny sack out onto the middle of the platform. "Herbie Stark sent this, it's potatoes mostly, and cabbages he was going to throw out of his store."

She takes the tiniest peek inside the sack and yes, there are potatoes there and some cabbages with soft brown leaves.

The engineer steps down out of his locomotive and comes along the side of the train rolling a cigarette. "Nice day again," he says with barely a glance at the sky. "You makin' out all right?"

"Hold it," the conductor says, as if he expects the train to move off by itself. "There's more." He climbs back into the passenger car and drags out a cardboard box heaped with groceries. "The church ladies said to drop this off," he says. "They told me make sure you get every piece of it, but I don't know how you'll ever get it down to the house through all that bush."

"She'll manage," the engineer says. He holds a lighted match under the ragged end of his cigarette until the loose tobacco blazes up. "She's been doing it—how long now?—must be six months."

The conductor pushes the cardboard box over against the sack of potatoes and stands back to wipe the sweat off his face. He glances at the engineer and they both smile a little and turn away. "Well," the engineer says, and heads back down the tracks and up into his locomotive.

The conductor tips his hat, says "Sorry," and climbs back into the empty passenger car. The train releases a long hiss and then moves slowly past her and down the tracks into the deep bush. She stands on the platform and looks after it a long while, as if a giant hand is pulling, slowly, a stay-stitching thread out of a fuzzy green cloth.

Snowbound by Ernest Lindner, 1937, linocut on paper.

The Wedding Gift

THOMAS RADDALL 1983

A land as big and as far north as Canada has to endure extremes of heat—and of cold. How is a newcomer to survive in a land where even the sea may sometimes freeze over? In this tale, set on the Atlantic coast in the winter of 1794, the author shows the terror of a newcomer—and the resourcefulness of a young woman in ensuring that their bitter winter journey together does not lead to hardship or to tragedy.

Nova Scotia, in 1794. Winter. Snow on the ground. Two feet of it in the woods, less by the shore, except in drifts against Port Marriott's barns and fences; but enough to set sleigh bells ringing through the town, enough to require a multitude of paths and burrows from doors to streets, to carpet the wharves and the decks of the shipping, and to trim the ships' yards with tippets of ermine. Enough to require fires roaring in the town's chimneys, and blue wood smoke hanging low over the roof tops in the still December air. Enough to squeal underfoot in the trodden places and to muffle the step everywhere else. Enough for the hunters, whose snow-shoes now could overtake the floundering moose and caribou. Even enough for the always-complaining loggers, whose ox sleds now could haul their cut from every part of the woods. But not enough, not nearly enough snow for Miss Kezia Barnes, who was going to Bristol Creek to marry Mr. Hathaway.

Kezia did not want to marry Mr. Hathaway. Indeed she had told Mr. and Mrs. Barclay in a tearful voice that she didn't want to marry anybody. But Mr. Barclay had taken snuff and said "Ha! Humph!" in the severe tone he used when he was displeased; and Mrs. Barclay had sniffed and said it was a very good match for her, and revolved the cold blue eyes in her fat moon face, and said Kezia must not be a little fool.

There were two ways of going to Bristol Creek. One was by sea, in one of the fishing sloops. But the preacher objected to that. He was a pallid young man lately sent out from England by Lady Huntingdon's Connexion, and seasick five weeks on the way. He held Mr. Barclay in some awe, for Mr. Barclay had the best pew in the meetinghouse and was the chief pillar of godliness in Port Marriott. But young Mr. Mears was firm on this point. He would go by road, he said, or not at all. Mr. Barclay had retorted "Ha! Humph!" The road was twenty miles of horse path through the woods, now deep in snow. Also the path began at Harper's Farm on the far side of the harbour, and Harper had but one horse.

"I shall walk," declared the preacher calmly, "and the young woman can ride."

Kezia had prayed for snow, storms of snow, to bury the trail and keep anyone from crossing the cape to Bristol Creek. But now they were setting out from Harper's Farm, with Harper's big brown horse, and all Kezia's prayers had gone for naught. Like any anxious lover, busy Mr. Hathaway had sent Black Sam overland on foot to find out what delayed his wedding, and now Sam's day-old tracks marked for Kezia the road to marriage.

She was a meek little thing, as became an orphan brought up as house-help in the Barclay home; but now she looked at the preacher and saw how young and helpless he looked so far from his native Yorkshire, and how ill-clad for this bitter trans-Atlantic weather, and she spoke up.

"You'd better take my shawl, sir. I don't need it. I've got Miss Julia's old riding cloak. And we'll go ride-and-tie."

"Ride and what?" murmured Mr. Mears.

"I'll ride a mile or so, then I'll get down and tie the horse to a tree and walk on. When you come up to the horse, you mount and ride a mile or so, passing me on the way, and you tie him and walk on. Like that. Ride-and-tie, ride-and-tie. The horse gets a rest between."

Young Mr. Mears nodded and took the proffered shawl absently. It was a black thing that matched his sober broadcloth coat and smallclothes, his black woollen stockings, and his round black hat. At Mr. Barclay's suggestion he had borrowed a pair of moose-hide moccasins for the journey. As he walked a prayer-book in his coat-skirts bumped the back of his legs.

At the top of the ridge above Harper's pasture, where the narrow path led off through gloomy hemlock woods, Kezia paused for a last look back across the harbour. In the morning sunlight the white roofs of the little lonely town resembled a tidal wave flung up by the sea and frozen as it broke against the dark pine forest to the west. Kezia sighed, and young Mr. Mears was surprised to see tears in her eyes.

She rode off ahead. The saddle was a man's, of course, awkward to ride modestly, woman-fashion. As soon as she was out of the preacher's sight she rucked her skirts and slid a leg over to the other stirrup. That was better. There was a pleasant sensation of freedom about it, too. For a moment she forgot that she was going to Bristol Creek, in finery second-hand from the Barclay girls, in a new linen shift and drawers that she had sewn herself in the light of the kitchen candles, in white cotton stockings and a bonnet and shoes from Mr. Barclay's store, to marry Mr. Hathaway.

The Barclays had done well for her from the time when, a skinny weeping creature of fourteen, she was taken into the Barclay household and, as Mrs. Barclay so often said, "treated more like one of my own than a bond-girl from the poorhouse." She had first choice of the clothing cast off by Miss Julia and Miss Clara. She was permitted to sit in the same room, and learn what she could, when the schoolmaster came to give private lessons to the Barclay girls. She waited on table, of course, and helped in the kitchen, and made beds, and dusted and scrubbed. But then she had been taught to spin and to sew and to knit. And she was permitted, indeed encouraged, to sit with the Barclays in the meetinghouse, at the convenient end of the pew, where she could worship the Barclays' God and assist with the Barclay wraps at the beginning and end of the service. And now, to complete her rewards, she had been granted the hand of a rejected Barclay suitor.

Mr. Hathaway was Barclay's agent at Bristol Creek, where he sold rum and gunpowder and corn meal and such things to the fishermen and hunters, and bought split cod—fresh, pickled or dry—and ran a small sawmill, and cut and shipped firewood by schooner to Port Marriott, and managed a farm, all for a salary of fifty pounds, Halifax currency, per year. Hathaway was a most capable fellow, Mr. Barclay often acknowledged. But when after fifteen capable years he came seeking a wife, and cast a sheep's eye first at Miss Julia, and then at Miss Clara, Mrs. Barclay observed with a sniff that Hathaway was looking a bit high.

So he was. The older daughter of Port Marriott's most prosperous merchant was even then receiving polite attentions from Mr. Gamage, the new collector of customs, and a connection of the Halifax Gamages, as Mrs. Barclay was fond of pointing out. And Miss Clara was going to Halifax in the spring to learn the gentle art of playing the pianoforte, and incidentally to display her charms to the naval and military young gentlemen who thronged the Halifax drawing-rooms. The dear girls laughed behind their hands whenever long solemn Mr. Hathaway came to town aboard one of the Barclay vessels and called at the big house under the elms. Mrs. Barclay bridled at Hathaway's presumption, but shrewd Mr. Barclay narrowed his little black eyes and took snuff and said "Ha! Humph!"

It was plain to Mr. Barclay that an emergency had arisen. Hathaway was a good man—in his place; and Hathaway must be kept content there, to go on making profit for Mr. Barclay at a cost of only £50 a year. 'Twas a pity Hathaway couldn't satisfy himself with one of the fishermen's girls at the Creek, but there 'twas. If Hathaway had set his mind on a town miss, then a town miss he must have; but she must be the right kind, the sort who would content herself and Hathaway at Bristol Creek and not go nagging the man to remove and try his capabilities elsewhere. At once Mr. Barclay thought of Kezia—dear little Kezzie. A colourless little creature but quiet and well-mannered and pious, and only twenty-two.

Mr. Hathaway was nearly forty and far from handsome, and he had a rather cold, seeking way about him—useful in business of course—that rubbed women the wrong way. Privately Mr. Barclay thought Hathaway lucky to get Kezia. But it was a nice match for the girl, better than anything she could have expected. He impressed that upon her and introduced the suitor from Bristol Creek. Mr. Hathaway spent two or three evenings courting Kezia in the kitchen—Kezia in a quite good gown of Miss Clara's, gazing out at the November moon on the snow, murmuring now and again in the tones of someone in a rather dismal trance, while the kitchen help listened behind one door and the Barclay girls giggled behind another.

The decision, reached mainly by the Barclays, was that Mr. Hathaway should come to Port Marriott aboard the packet schooner on December twenty-third, to be married in the Barclay parlour and then take his bride home for Christmas. But an unforeseen circumstance had changed all this. The circumstance was a ship, "from Mogador in Barbary" as Mr. Barclay wrote afterwards in the salvage claim, driven off her course by gales and wrecked at the very entrance to Bristol Creek. She was a valuable wreck, laden with such queer things as goatskins in pickle, almonds, wormseed, pomegranate skins, and gum arabic, and capable Mr. Hathaway had lost no time in salvage for the benefit of his employer.

As a result he could not come to Port Marriott for a wedding or anything else. A storm might blow up at any time and demolish this fat prize. He dispatched a note by Black Sam, urging Mr. Barclay to send Kezia and the preacher by return. It was not the orthodox note of an impatient sweetheart but it said that he had moved into his new house by the Creek and found i "extream empty lacking a woman," and it suggested delicately that while his days were full, the nights were dull.

Kezia was no judge of distance. She rode for what she considered a reasonable time and then slid off and tied the brown horse to a maple tree beside the path. She had brought a couple of lamp wicks to tie about her shoes, to keep them from coming off in the snow, and she set out afoot in the big splayed tracks of Black Sam. The soft snow came almost to her knees in places and she lifted her skirts high. The path was no wider than the span of a man's arms, cut out with axes years before. She stumbled over a concealed stump from time to time, and the huckleberry bushes dragged at her cloak, but the effort warmed her. It had been cold, sitting on the horse with the wind blowing up her legs.

After a time the preacher overtook her, riding awkwardly and holding the reins in a nervous grip. The stirrups were too short for his long black-stockinged legs. He called out cheerfully as he passed, "Are you all right, Miss?" She nodded, standing aside with her back to a tree. When he disappeared ahead, with a last flutter of black shawl tassels in the wind, she picked up her skirts and went on. The path climbed and dropped monotonously over a succession of wooded ridges. Here and there in a hollow she heard water running, and the creak of frosty poles underfoot, and knew she was crossing a small stream, and once the trail ran across a wide swamp on half-rotten corduroy, wind-swept and bare of snow.

She found the horse tethered clumsily not far ahead, and the tracks of the preacher going on. She had to lead the horse to a stump so she could mount, and when she passed Mr. Mears again she called out, "Please, sir, next time leave the horse by a stump or a rock so I can get on." In his quaint old-country accent he murmured, "I'm very sorry," and gazed down at the snow. She forgot she was riding astride until she had passed him, and then she flushed, and gave the indignant horse a cut of the switch. Next time she remembered and swung her right leg back where it should be, and tucked the skirts modestly about her ankles; but young Mr. Mears looked down at the snow anyway, and after that she did not trouble to shift when she overtook him.

The ridges became steeper, and the streams roared under the ice and snow in the swales. They emerged upon the high tableland between Port Marriott and Bristol Creek, a gusty wilderness of young hardwood scrub struggling up amongst the grey snags of an old forest fire, and now that they were out of the gloomy softwoods they could see a stretch of sky. It was blue-grey and forbidding, and the wind whistling up from the invisible sea felt raw on the cheek. At their next meeting Kezia said, "It's going to snow."

She had no knowledge of the trail but she guessed that they were not much more than halfway across the cape. On this high barren the track was no longer straight and clear, it meandered amongst the meagre hardwood clumps where the path-makers had not bothered to cut, and only Black Sam's footprints really marked it for her unaccustomed eyes. The preacher nodded vaguely at her remark. The woods, like everything else about his chosen mission field, were new and very interesting, and he could not understand the alarm in her voice. He looked confidently at Black Sam's tracks.

Kezia tied the horse farther on and began her spell of walking. Her shoes were solid things, the kind of shoes Mr. Barclay invoiced as "a Common Strong sort, for women, Five Shillings"; but the snow worked into them and melted and saturated the leather. Her feet were numb every time she slid down from the horse and it took several minutes of stumbling through the snow to bring back an aching warmth. Beneath her arm she clutched the small bundle which contained all she had in the world—two flannel nightgowns, a shift of linen, three pairs of stout wool stockings—and of course Mr. Barclay's wedding gift for Mr. Hathaway.

Now as she plunged along she felt the first sting of snow on her face and looking up, saw the stuff borne on the wind in small hard pellets that fel amongst the bare hardwoods and set up a whisper everywhere. When Mr Mears rode up to her the snow was thick in their faces, like flung salt.

"It's a nor'easter!" she cried up to him. She knew the meaning of snow from the sea. She had been born in a fishing village down the coast.

"Yes," mumbled the preacher, and drew a fold of the shawl about his face He disappeared. She struggled on, gasping, and after what seemed a tremendous journey came upon him standing alone and bewildered, looking off somewhere to the right.

"The horse!" he shouted. "I got off him, and before I could fasten the rein some snow fell off a branch—startled him, you know—and he ran off, ove that way." He gestured with a mittened hand. "I must fetch him back," h added confusedly.

"No!" Kezia cried. "Don't you try. You'd only get lost. So would I. Oh dear! This is awful. We'll have to go on, the best we can."

He was doubtful. The horse tracks looked very plain. But Kezia wa looking at Black Sam's tracks, and tugging his arm. He gave in, and the struggled along for half an hour or so. Then the last trace of the old footprints vanished.

"What shall we do now?" the preacher asked, astonished.

"I don't know," whispered Kezia, and leaned against a dead pine stub in an attitude of weariness and indifference that dismayed him.

"We must keep moving, my dear, mustn't we? I mean, we can't stay here."

"Can't stay here," she echoed.

"Down there—a hollow, I think. I see some hemlock trees, or are they pines?—I'm never quite sure. Shelter, anyway."

"Shelter," muttered Kezia.

He took her by the hand and like a pair of lost children they dragged their steps into the deep snow of the hollow. The trees were tall spruces, a thick bunch in a ravine, where they had escaped the old fire. A stream thundered amongst them somewhere. There was no wind in this place, only the fine snow whirling thickly down between the trees like a sediment from the storm overhead.

"Look!" cried Mr. Mears. A hut loomed out of the whiteness before them, a small structure of moss-chinked logs with a roof of poles and birch-bark. It had an abandoned look. Long streamers of moss hung out between the logs. On the roof shreds of birch-bark wavered gently in the drifting snow. The door stood half open and a thin drift of snow lay along the split-pole floor. Instinctively Kezia went to the stone hearth. There were old ashes sodden with rain down the chimney and now frozen to a cake.

"Have you got flint and steel?" she asked. She saw in his eyes something dazed and forlorn. He shook his head, and she was filled with a sudden anger, not so much at him as at Mr. Barclay and that—Hathaway, and all the rest of mankind. They ruled the world and made such a sorry mess of it. In a small fury she began to rummage about the hut.

There was a crude bed of poles and brushwood by the fireplace—brushwood so old that only a few brown needles clung to the twigs. A rough bench whittled from a pine log, with round birch sticks for legs. A broken earthenware pot in a corner. In another some ash-wood frames such as trappers used for stretching skins. Nothing else. The single window was covered with a stretched moose-bladder, cracked and dry rotten, but it still let in some daylight while keeping out the snow.

She scooped up the snow from the floor with her mittened hands, throwing it outside, and closed the door carefully, dropping the bar into place, as if she could shut out and bar the cold in such a fashion. The air inside was frigid. Their breath hung visible in the dim light from the window. Young Mr. Mears dropped on his wet knees and began to pray in a loud voice. His face was pinched with cold and his teeth rattled as he prayed. He was a pitiable object.

"Prayers won't keep you warm," said Kezia crossly.

He looked up, amazed at the change in her. She had seemed such a meek little thing. Kezia was surprised at herself, and surprisingly she went on, "You'd far better take off those wet moccasins and stockings and shake the snow out of your clothes." She set the example, vigorously shaking out her skirts and Miss Julia's cloak, and she turned her small back on him and took off her own shoes and stockings, and pulled on dry stockings from her bundle. She threw him a pair.

"Put those on."

He looked at them and at his large feet, hopelessly.

"I'm afraid they wouldn't go on."

She tossed him one of her flannel nightgowns. "Then take off your stockings and wrap your feet and legs in that."

He obeyed, in an embarrassed silence. She rolled her eyes upward, for his modesty's sake, and saw a bundle on one of the low rafters—the late owner's bedding, stowed away from mice. She stood on the bench and pulled down three bearskins, marred with bullet holes. A rank and dusty smell arose in the cold. She considered the find gravely.

"You take them," Mr. Mears said gallantly. "I shall be quite all right."

"You'll be dead by morning, and so shall I," she answered vigorously, "if you don't do what I say. We've got to roll up in these."

"Together?" he cried in horror.

"Of course! To keep each other warm. It's the only way."

She spread the skins on the floor, hair uppermost, one overlapping another, and dragged the flustered young man down beside her, clutched him in her arms, and rolled with him, over, and over again, so that they became a single shapeless heap in the corner farthest from the draft between door and chimney.

"Put your arms around me," commanded the new Kezia, and he obeyed.

"Now," she said, "you can pray. God helps those that help themselves."

He prayed aloud for a long time, and privately called upon heaven to witness the purity of his thoughts in this strange and shocking situation. He said "Amen" at last; and "Amen," echoed Kezia, piously.

They lay silent a long time, breathing on each other's necks and hearing their own hearts—poor Mr. Mears' fluttering in an agitated way, Kezia's as steady as a clock. A delicious warmth crept over them. They relaxed in each other's arms. Outside, the storm hissed in the spruce tops and set up an occasional cold moan in the cracked clay chimney. The down-swirling snow brushed softly against the bladder pane.

"I'm warm now," murmured Kezia. "Are you?"

"Yes. How long must we stay here like this?"

"Till the storm's over, of course. Tomorrow, probably. Nor'easters usually blow themselves out in a day and a night, 'specially when they come up sharp, like this one. Are you hungry?"

"No."

"Abigail—that's the black cook at Barclays'—gave me bread and cheese in a handkerchief. I've got it in my bundle. Mr. Barclay thought we ought to reach Bristol Creek by supper time, but Nabby said I must have a bite to eat on the road. She's a good kind thing, old Nabby. Sure you're not hungry?"

"Quite. I feel somewhat fatigued but not hungry."

"Then we'll eat the bread and cheese for breakfast. Have you got a watch?"

"No, I'm sorry. They cost such a lot of money. In Lady Huntingdon's Connexion we—"

"Oh well, it doesn't matter. It must be about four o'clock—the light's getting dim. Of course, the dark comes very quick in a snowstorm."

"Dark," echoed young Mr. Mears drowsily. Kezia's hair, washed last night for the wedding journey, smelled pleasant so close to his face. It reminded him of something. He went to sleep dreaming of his mother, with his face snug in the curve of Kezia's neck and shoulder, and smiling, and muttering words that Kezia could not catch. After a time she kissed his cheek. It seemed a very natural thing to do.

Soon she was dozing herself, and dreaming, too; but her dreams were full of forbidding faces—Mr. Barclay's, Mrs. Barclay's, Mr. Hathaway's; especially Mr. Hathaway's. Out of a confused darkness Mr. Hathaway's hard acquisitive gaze searched her shrinking flesh like a cold wind. Then she was shuddering by the kitchen fire at Barclays', accepting Mr. Hathaway's courtship and wishing she was dead. In the midst of that sickening wooing she wakened sharply.

It was quite dark in the hut. Mr. Mears was breathing quietly against her throat. But there was a sound of heavy steps outside, muffled in the snow and somehow felt rather than heard. She shook the young man and he wakened with a start, clutching her convulsively.

"Sh-h-h!" she warned. "Something's moving outside." She felt him stiffen.

"Bears?" he whispered.

Silly! thought Kezia. People from the old country could think of nothing but bears in the woods. Besides, bears holed up in winter. A caribou, perhaps. More likely a moose. Caribou moved inland before this, to the wide mossy bogs up the river, away from the coastal storms. Again the sound.

"There!" hissed the preacher. Their hearts beat rapidly together.

"The door—you fastened it, didn't you?"

"Yes," she said. Suddenly she knew.

"Unroll, quick!" she cried ... "No, not this way—your way."

They unrolled, ludicrously, and the girl scrambled up and ran across the floor in her stockinged feet, and fumbled with the rotten door-bar. Mr. Mears attempted to follow but he tripped over the nightgown still wound around his feet, and fell with a crash. He was up again in a moment, catching up the clumsy wooden bench for a weapon, his bare feet slapping on the icy floor. He tried to shoulder her aside, crying "Stand back! Leave it to me!" and waving the bench uncertainly in the darkness.

She laughed excitedly. "Silly!" she said. "It's the horse." She flung the door open. In the queer ghostly murk of a night filled with snow they beheld a large dark shape. The shape whinnied softly and thrust a long face into the doorway. Mr. Mears dropped the bench, astonished.

"He got over his fright and followed us here somehow," Kezia said, and laughed again. She put her arms about the snowy head and laid her face against it.

"Good horse! Oh, good, good horse!"

"What are you going to do?" the preacher murmured over her shoulder. After the warmth of their nest in the furs they were shivering in this icy atmosphere.

"Bring him in, of course. We can't leave him out in the storm." She caught the bridle and urged the horse inside with expert clucking sounds. The animal hesitated, but fear of the storm and a desire for shelter and company decided him. In he came, tramping ponderously on the split-pole floor. The preacher closed and barred the door.

"And now?" he asked.

"Back to the furs. Quick! It's awful cold."

Rolled in the furs once more, their arms went about each other instinctively, and the young man's face found the comfortable nook against Kezia's soft throat. But sleep was difficult after that. The horse whinnied gently from time to time, and stamped about the floor. The decayed poles crackled dangerously under his hoofs whenever he moved, and Kezia trembled, thinking he might break through and frighten himself, and flounder about till he tumbled the crazy hut about their heads. She called out to him "Steady, boy! Steady!"

It was a long night. The pole floor made its irregularities felt through the thickness of fur; and because there seemed nowhere to put their arms but about each other the flesh became cramped, and spread its protest along the bones. They were stiff and sore when the first light of morning stained the window. They unrolled and stood up thankfully, and tramped up and down the floor, threshing their arms in an effort to fight off the gripping cold. Kezia undid her bundle in a corner and brought forth Nabby's bread and cheese, and they ate it sitting together on the edge of the brushwood bed with the skins about their shoulders. Outside the snow had ceased.

"We must set off at once," the preacher said. "Mr. Hathaway will be anxious."

Kezia was silent. She did not move, and he looked at her curiously. She appeared very fresh, considering the hardships of the previous day and night. He passed a hand over his cheeks and thought how unclean he must appear in her eyes with this stubble on his pale face.

"Mr. Hathaway—" he began again.

"I'm not going to Mr. Hathaway," Kezia said quietly.

"But—the wedding!"

"There'll be no wedding. I don't want to marry Mr. Hathaway. 'Twas Mr. Hathaway's idea, and Mr. and Mrs. Barclay's. They wanted me to marry him."

"What will the Barclays say, my dear?"

She shrugged. "I've been their bond-girl ever since I was fourteen, but I'm not a slave like poor black Nabby, to be handed over, body and soul, whenever it suits."

"Your soul belongs to God," said Mr. Mears devoutly.

"And my body belongs to me."

He was a little shocked at this outspokenness but he said gently, "Of course. To give oneself in marriage without true affection would be an offence in the sight of Heaven. But what will Mr. Hathaway say?"

"Well, to begin with, he'll ask where I spent the night, and I'll have to tell the truth. I'll have to say I bundled with you in a hut in the woods."

"Bundled?"

"A custom the people brought with them from Connecticut when they came to settle in Nova Scotia. Poor folk still do it. Sweethearts, I mean. It saves fire and candles when you're courting on a winter evening. It's harmless—they keep their clothes on, you see, like you and me—but Mr. Barclay and the other Methody people are terrible set against it. Mr. Barclay got old Mr. Mings—he's the Methody preacher that died last year—to make a sermon against it. Mr. Mings said bundling was an invention of the devil."

"Then if you go back to Mr. Barclay—"

"He'll ask me the same question and I'll have to give him the same answer. I couldn't tell a lie, could I?" She turned a pair of round blue eyes and met his embarrassed gaze.

"No! No, you mustn't lie. Whatever shall we do?" he murmured in a dazed voice. Again she was silent, looking modestly down her small nose.

"It's so very strange," he floundered. "This country—there are so many things I don't know, so many things to learn. You—I—we shall have to tell the truth, of course. Doubtless I can find a place in the Lord's service somewhere else, but what about you, poor girl?"

"I heard say the people at Scrod Harbour want a preacher."

"But—the tale would follow me, wouldn't it, my dear? This—er—bundling with a young woman?"

"'Twouldn't matter if the young woman was your wife."

"Eh?" His mouth fell open. He was like an astonished child, for all his preacher's clothes and the new beard on his jaws.

"I'm a good girl," Kezia said, inspecting her foot. "I can read and write, and know all the tunes in the psalter. And—and you need someone to look after you."

He considered the truth of that. Then he murmured uncertainly, "We'd be very poor, my dear. The Connexion gives some support, but of course—"

"I've always been poor," Kezia said. She sat very still but her cold fingers writhed in her lap.

He did something then that made her want to cry. He took hold of her hands and bowed his head and kissed them.

"It's strange—I don't even know your name, my dear."

"It's Kezia—Kezia Barnes."

He said quietly, "You're a brave girl, Kezia Barnes, and I shall try to be a good husband to you. Shall we go?"

"Hadn't you better kiss me, first?" Kezia said faintly.

He put his lips awkwardly to hers; and then, as if the taste of her clean mouth itself provided strength and purpose, he kissed her again, and firmly. She threw her arms about his neck.

"Oh, Mr. Mears!"

How little he knew about everything! He hadn't even known enough to wear two or three pairs of stockings inside those roomy moccasins, nor to carry a pair of dry ones. Yesterday's wet stockings were lying like sticks on the frosty floor. She showed him how to knead the hard-frozen moccasins into softness, and while he worked at the stiff leather she tore up one of her wedding bed-shirts and wound the flannel strips about his legs and feet. It looked very queer when she had finished, and they both laughed.

They were chilled to the bone when they set off, Kezia on the horse and the preacher walking ahead, holding the reins. When they regained the slope where they had lost the path, Kezia said, "The sun rises somewhere between east and southeast, this time of year. Keep it on your left shoulder a while. That will take us back towards Port Marriott."

When they came to the green timber she told him to shift the sun to his left eye.

"Have you changed your mind?" he asked cheerfully. The exercise had warmed him.

"No, but the sun moves across the sky."

"Ah! What a wise little head it is!"

They came over a ridge of mixed hemlock and hardwood and looked upon a long swale full of bare hackmatacks.

"Look!" the girl cried. The white slot of the axe path showed clearly in the trees at the foot of the swale, and again where it entered the dark mass of the pines beyond.

"Praise the Lord!" said Mr. Mears.

When at last they stood in the trail, Kezia slid down from the horse.

"No!" Mr. Mears protested.

"Ride-and-tie," she said firmly. "That's the way we came, and that's the way we'll go. Besides, I want to get warm."

He climbed up clumsily and smiled down at her.

"What shall we do when we get to Port Marriott, my dear?"

"Get the New Light preacher to marry us, and catch the packet for Scrod Harbour."

He nodded and gave a pull at his broad hat brim. She thought of everything. A splendid helpmeet for the world's wilderness. He saw it all very humbly now as a dispensation of Providence.

Kezia watched him out of sight. Then, swiftly, she undid her bundle and took out the thing that had lain there (and on her conscience) through the night—the tinderbox—Mr. Barclay's wedding gift to Mr. Hathaway. She flung it into the woods and walked on, skirts lifted, in the track of the horse, humming a psalm tune to the silent trees and the snow.

Winter Dog

ALISTAIR MACLEOD 1986

Canada may be a land of immigrants, but it is also a land of migrants — people who have left one of its great provinces to live in another. For many, their migration can create as big a sense of loss as immigrants can feel when they recall their homeland. In this tale, the sight of a dog playing with children in the modern ease of a temporarily snowbound inland city reminds the exiled narrator of his own childhood. Memories return of when he lived in a far harder part of Canada, the Atlantic Maritimes, and of when he and his dog once had their love and loyalty put to the harshest test at the cruellest time of the year.

I am writing this in December, in the period close to Christmas, and three days after the first snowfall in this region of southwestern Ontario. The snow came quietly in the night or in the early morning. When we went to bed near midnight, there was none at all. Then early in the morning we heard the children singing Christmas songs from their rooms across the hall. It was very dark and I rolled over to check the time. It was 4:30 a.m. One of them must have awakened and looked out the window to find the snow and then eagerly awakened the others. They are half crazed by the promise of Christmas, and the discovery of the snow is an unexpectedly giddy surprise. There was no snow promised for this area, not even yesterday.

"What are you doing?" I call, although it is obvious.

"Singing Christmas songs," they shout back with equal obviousness, "because it snowed."

"Try to be quiet," I say, "or you'll wake the baby."

"She's already awake," they say. "She's listening to our singing. She likes it. Can we go out and make a snowman?"

I roll from my bed and go to the window. The neighbouring houses are muffled in snow and silence and there are as yet no lights in any of them. The snow has stopped falling and its whitened quietness reflects the shadows of the night.

"This snow is no good for snowmen," I say. "It is too dry."

"How can snow be dry?" asks a young voice. Then an older one says, "Well, then can we go out and make the first tracks?"

Survivor Wandering by David Blackwood, 1969, etching.

They take my silence for consent and there are great sounds of rustling and giggling as they go downstairs to touch the light switches and rummage and jostle for coats and boots.

"What on earth is happening?" asks my wife from her bed. "What are they doing?"

"They are going outside to make the first tracks in the snow," I say. "It snowed quite heavily last night."

"What time is it?"

"Shortly after 4:30."

"Oh."

We ourselves have been quite nervous and restless for the past weeks. We have been troubled by illness and uncertainty in those we love far away on Canada's east coast. We have already considered and rejected driving the fifteen hundred miles. Too far, too uncertain, too expensive, fickle weather, the complications of transporting Santa Claus.

Instead, we sleep uncertainly and toss in unbidden dreams. We jump when the phone rings after 10:00 p.m. and are then reassured by the distant voices.

"First of all, there is nothing wrong," they say. "Things are just the same."

Sometimes we make calls ourselves, even to the hospital in Halifax, and are surprised at the voices which answer.

"I just got here this afternoon from Newfoundland. I'm going to try to stay a week. He seems better today. He's sleeping now."

At other times we receive calls from farther west, from Edmonton and Calgary and Vancouver. People hoping to find objectivity in the most subjective of situations. Strung out in uncertainty across the time zones from British Columbia to Newfoundland.

Within our present city, people move and consider possibilities:

If he dies tonight we'll leave right away. Can you come?

We will have to drive as we'll never get air reservations at this time.

I'm not sure if my car is good enough. I'm always afraid of the mountains near Cabano.

If we were stranded in Rivière du Loup we would be worse off than being here. It would be too far for anyone to come and get us.

My car will go but I'm not so sure I can drive it all the way. My eyes are not so good anymore, especially at night in drifting snow.

Perhaps there'll be no drifting snow.

There's always drifting snow.

We'll take my car if you'll drive it. We'll have to drive straight through.

John phoned and said he'll give us his car if we want it or he'l drive—either his own car or someone else's.

He drinks too heavily, especially for long-distance driving, and at this tim of year. He's been drinking ever since this news began.

He drinks because he cares. It's just the way he is.

Not everybody drinks.

Not everybody cares, and if he gives you his word, he'll never drink until h gets there. We all know that.

But so far nothing has happened. Things seem to remain the same.

Through the window and out on the white plane of the snow, the silen laughing children now appear. They move in their muffled clothes lik mummers on the whitest of stages. They dance and gesture noiselessl flopping their arms in parodies of heavy, happy, earthbound birds. They hav been warned by the eldest to be aware of the sleeping neighbours so the cavort only in pantomime, sometimes raising mittened hands to their mout to suppress their joyous laughter. They dance and prance in the moonligh tossing snow in one another's direction, tracing out various shapes an initials, forming lines which snake across the previously unmarked whit ness. All of it in silence, unknown and unseen and unheard to t neighbouring world. They seem unreal even to me, their father, standing his darkened window. It is almost as if they have danced out of the world folklore like happy elves who cavort and mimic and caper through the priva hours of this whitened dark, only to vanish with the coming of the morning light and leaving only the signs of their activities behind. I am tempted check the recently vacated beds to confirm what perhaps I think I know

Then out of the corner of my eye I see him. The golden collie-like dog. H appears almost as if from the wings of the stage or as a figure newly noticed the lower corner of a winter painting. He sits quietly and watches the playf scene before him and then, as if responding to a silent invitation, bounds in its midst. The children chase him in frantic circles, falling and rolling as doubles back and darts and dodges between their legs and through th outstretched arms. He seizes a mitt loosened from its owner's hand, a tosses it happily in the air and then snatches it back into his jaws an insta before it reaches the ground and seconds before the tumbling bodies fall the emptiness of its expected destination. He races to the edge of the scene a lies facing them, holding the mitt tantalizingly between his paws, and then they dash towards him, he leaps forward again, tossing and catching it before him and zig-zagging through them as the Sunday football player might return the much sought-after ball. After he has gone through and eluded them all, he looks back over his shoulder and again, like an elated athlete, tosses the mitt high in what seems like an imaginary end zone. Then he seizes it once more and lopes in a wide circle around his pursuers, eventually coming closer and closer to them until once more their stretching hands are able to actually touch his shoulders and back and haunches, although he continues always to wriggle free. He is touched but never captured, which is the nature of the game. Then he is gone. As suddenly as he came. I strain my eyes in the direction of the adjoining street, towards the house where I have often seen him, always within a yard enclosed by woven links of chain. I see the flash of his silhouette, outlined perhaps against the snow or the light cast by the street lamps or the moon. It arcs upwards and seems to hang for an instant high above the top of the fence and then it descends on the other side. He lands on his shoulder in a fluff of snow and with a half roll regains his feet and vanishes within the shadow of his owner's house.

"What are you looking at?" asks my wife.

"That golden collie-like dog from the other street was just playing with the children in the snow."

"But he's always in that fenced-in yard."

"I guess not always. He jumped the fence just now and went back in. I guess the owners and the rest of us think he's fenced in but he knows he's not. He probably comes out every night and leads an exciting life. I hope they don't see his tracks or they'll probably begin to chain him."

"What are the children doing?"

"They look tired now from chasing the dog. They'll probably soon be back in. I think I'll go downstairs and wait for them and make myself a cup of coffee."

"Okay."

I look once more towards the fenced-in yard but the dog is nowhere to be seen.

I first saw such a dog when I was twelve and he came as a pup of about two months in a crate to the railroad station which was about eight miles from where we lived. Someone must have phoned or dropped in to say: "Your dog's at the station."

He had come to Cape Breton in response to a letter and a cheque which my father had sent to Morrisburg, Ontario. We had seen the ads for "cattle collie dogs" in the *Family Herald*, which was the farm newspaper of the time, and we were in need of a good young working dog.

His crate was clean and neat and there was still a supply of dog biscuits with him and a can in the corner to hold water. The baggage handlers had looked after him well on the trip east, and he appeared in good spirits. He had a white collar and chest and four rather large white paws and a small white blaze on his forehead. The rest of him was a fluffy, golden brown, although his eyebrows and the tips of his ears as well as the end of his tail were darker, tingeing almost to black. When he grew to his full size the blackish shadings became really black, and although he had the long, heavy coat of a collie, it was in certain areas more grey than gold. He was also taller than the average collie and with a deeper chest. He seemed to be at least part German Shepherd.

It was winter when he came and we kept him in the house where he slept behind the stove in a box lined with an old coat. Our other dogs slept mostly in the stables or outside in the lees of woodpiles or under porches or curled up on the banking of the house. We seemed to care more for him because he was smaller and it was winter and he was somehow like a visitor; and also because more was expected of him and also perhaps because we had paid money for him and thought about his coming for some time—like a "planned" child. Sceptical neighbours and relatives who thought the idea of paying money for a dog was rather exotic or frivolous would ask: "Is that your Ontario dog" or "Do you think your Ontario dog will be any good?"

He turned out to be no good at all and no one knew why. Perhaps it was because of the suspected German Shepherd blood. But he could not "get the hang of it." Although we worked him and trained him as we had other dogs, he seemed always to bring panic instead of order and to make things worse instead of better. He became a "head dog," which meant that instead of working behind the cattle he lunged at their heads, impeding them from any forward motion and causing them to turn in endless, meaningless bewildered circles. On the few occasions when he did go behind them, he was "rough", which meant that instead of being a floating, nipping, suggestive presence, he actually bit them and caused them to gallop, which was another sin. Sometimes in the summer the milk cows suffering from his misunderstood pursuit would jam pell mell into the stable, tossing their wide horns in fear, and with their great sides heaving and perspiring while down their legs and tails the wasted milk ran in rivulets mingling with the blood caused by his slashing wounds. He was, it was said, "worse than nothing."

Gradually everyone despaired, although he continued to grow grey and golden and was, as everyone agreed, a "beautiful-looking dog."

He was also tremendously strong and in the winter months I would hitch him to a sleigh which he pulled easily and willingly on almost any kind of surface. When he was harnessed I used to put a collar around his neck and attach a light line to it so that I might have some minimum control over him, but it was hardly ever needed. He would pull home the Christmas tree or the bag of flour or the deer which was shot far back in the woods; and when we visited our winter snares he would pull home the gunnysacks which contained the partridges and rabbits which we gathered. He would also pull us, especially on the flat windswept stretches of land beside the sea. There the snow was never really deep and the water that oozed from a series of fresh-water springs and ponds contributed to a glaze of ice and crisply crusted snow which the sleigh runners seemed to sing over without ever breaking through. He would begin with an easy lope and then increase his swiftness until both he and the sleigh seemed to touch the surface at only irregular intervals. He would stretch out then with his ears flattened against his head and his shoulders bunching and contracting in the rhythm of his speed. Behind him on the sleigh we would cling tenaciously to the wooden slats as the particles of ice and snow dislodged by his nails hurtled towards our faces. We would avert our heads and close our eyes and the wind stung so sharply that the difference between freezing and burning could not be known. He would do that until late in the afternoon when it was time to return home and begin our chores.

On the sunny winter Sunday that I am thinking of, I planned to visit my snares. There seemed no other children around that afternoon and the adults were expecting relatives. I harnessed the dog to the sleigh, opened the door of the house and shouted that I was going to look at my snares. We began to climb the hill behind the house on our way to the woods when we looked back and out towards the sea. The "big ice", which was what we called the major pack of drift ice, was in solidly against the shore and stretched out beyond the range of vision. It had not been "in" yesterday, although for the past weeks we had seen it moving offshore, sometimes close and sometimes distant, depending on the winds and tides. The coming of the big ice marked the official beginning of the coldest part of winter. It was mostly drift ice from the

Arctic and Labrador, although some of it was fresh-water ice from the estuary of the St. Lawrence. It drifted down with the dropping temperatures, bringing its own mysterious coldness and stretching for hundreds of miles in craters and pans, sometimes in grotesque shapes and sometimes in dazzling architectural forms. It was blue and white and sometimes grey and at other times a dazzling emerald green.

The dog and I changed our direction towards the sea, to find what the ice might yield. Our land had always been beside the sea and we had always gone towards it to find newness and the extraordinary; and over the years we, as others along the coast, had found quite a lot, although never the pirate chests of gold which were supposed to abound or the reasons for the mysterious lights that our elders still spoke of and persisted in seeing. But kegs of rum had washed up, and sometimes bloated horses and various fishing paraphernalia and valuable timber and furniture from foundered ships. The door of my room was apparently the galley door from a ship called the *Judith Franklin* which was wrecked during the early winter in which my great-grandfather was building his house. My grandfather told of how they had heard the cries and seen the lights as the ship neared the rocks and of how they had run down in the dark and tossed lines to the people while tying themselves to trees on the shore. All were saved, including women clinging to small children. The next day the builders of the new house went down to the shore and salvaged what they could from the wreckage of the vanquished ship. A sort of symbolic marriage of the new and the old: doors and shelving, stairways, hatches, wooden chests and trunks and various glass figurines and lanterns which were miraculously never broken.

People came too. The dead as well as the living. Bodies of men swept overboard and reported lost at sea and the bodies of men still crouched within the shelter of their boats' broken bows. And sometimes in late winter young sealers who had quit their vessels would walk across the ice and come to our doors. They were usually very young — some still in their teens — and had signed on for jobs they could not or no longer wished to handle. They were often disoriented and did not know where they were, only that they had seen land and had decided to walk towards it. They were often frostbitten and with little money and uncertain as to how they might get to Halifax. The dog and I walked towards the ice upon the sea.

Sometimes it was hard to "get on" the ice, which meant that at the point where the pack met the shore there might be open water or irregularities caused by the indentations of the coastline or the workings of the tides and currents, but for us on that day there was no difficulty at all. We were "on" easily and effortlessly and enthused in our new adventure. For the first mile there was nothing but the vastness of the white expanse. We came to a clear stretch where the ice was as smooth and unruffled as that of an indoor arena and I knelt on the sleigh while the dog loped easily along. Gradually the ice changed to an uneven terrain of pressure ridges and hummocks, making it impossible to ride farther; and then suddenly, upon rounding a hummock, I saw the perfect seal. At first I thought it was alive, as did the dog who stopped so suddenly in his tracks that the sleigh almost collided with his legs. The hackles on the back of his neck rose and he growled in the dangerous way he was beginning to develop. But the seal was dead, yet facing us in a frozen perfection that was difficult to believe. There was a light powder of snow over its darker coat and a delicate rime of frost still formed the outline of its whiskers. Its eyes were wide open and it stared straight ahead towards the land. Even now in memory it seems more real than reality—as if it were transformed by frozen art into something more arresting than life itself. The way the sudden seal in the museum exhibit freezes your eyes with the touch of truth. Immediately I wanted to take it home.

It was frozen solidly in a base of ice so I began to look for something that might serve as a pry. I let the dog out of his harness and hung the sleigh and harness on top of the hummock to mark the place and began my search. Some distance away I found a pole about twelve feet long. It is always surprising to find such things on the ice field but they are, often amazingly, there, almost in the same way that you might find a pole floating in the summer ocean. Unpredictable but possible. I took the pole back and began my work. The dog went off on explorations of his own.

Although it was firmly frozen, the task did not seem impossible and by inserting the end of the pole under first one side and then the other and working from the front to the back, it was possible to cause a gradual loosening. I remember thinking how very warm it was because I was working hard and perspiring heavily. When the dog came back he was uneasy, and I realized it was starting to snow a bit but I was almost done. He sniffed with disinterest at the seal and began to whine a bit, which was something he did not often do. Finally, after another quarter of an hour, I was able to roll my trophy onto the sleigh and with the dog in harness we set off. We had gone perhaps two hundred yards when the seal slid free. I took the dog and the sleigh back and once again managed to roll the seal on. This time I took the line from the dog's collar and tied the seal to the sleigh, reasoning that the dog would go home anyway and there would be no need to guide him. My fingers were numb as I tried to fasten the awkward knots and the dog began to whine and rear. When I gave the command he bolted forward and I clung at the back of the sleigh to the seal. The snow was heavier now and blowing in my face but we were moving rapidly and when we came to the stretch of arena-like ice we skimmed across it almost like an iceboat, the profile of the frozen seal at the front of the sleigh like those figures at the prows of Viking ships. At the very end of the smooth stretch, we went through. From my position at the end of the sleigh I felt him drop almost before I saw him, and rolled backwards seconds before the sleigh and seal followed him into the blackness of the water. He went under once carried by his own momentum but surfaced almost immediately with his head up and his paws scrambling at the icy, jagged edge of the hole; but when the weight and momentum of the sleigh and its burden struck, he went down again, this time out of sight.

I realized we had struck a "seam" and that the stretch of smooth ice had been deceivingly and temporarily joined to the rougher ice near the shore and now was in the process of breaking away. I saw the widening line before me and jumped to the other side just as his head miraculously came up once more. I lay on my stomach and grabbed his collar in both my hands and then in a moment of panic did not know what to do. I could feel myself sliding towards him and the darkness of the water and was aware of the weight that pulled me forward and down. I was also aware of his razor-sharp claws flailing violently before my face and knew that I might lose my eyes. And I was aware that his own eyes were bulging from their sockets and that he might think I was trying to choke him and might lunge and slash my face with his teeth in desperation. I knew all of this but somehow did nothing about it; it seemed almost simpler to hang on and be drawn into the darkness of the gently slopping water, seeming to slop gently in spite of all the agitation. Then suddenly he was free, scrambling over my shoulder and dragging the sleigh behind him. The seal surfaced again, buoyed up perhaps by the physics of its frozen body or the nature of its fur. Still looking more genuine than it could have in life, its snout and head broke the open water and it seemed to look at us curiously for an instant before it vanished permanently beneath the ice. The loose and badly tied knots had apparently not held when the sleigh was in a near-vertical position and we were saved by the ineptitude of my own numbed fingers. We had been spared for a future time.

He lay gasping and choking for a moment, coughing up the icy salt water, and then almost immediately his coat began to freeze. I realized then how cold I was myself and that even in the moments I had been lying on the ice, my clothes had begun to adhere to it. My earlier heated perspiration was now a cold rime upon my body and I imagined it outlining me there, beneath my clothes, in a sketch of frosty white. I got on the sleigh once more and crouched low as he began to race towards home. His coat was freezing fast, and as he ran the individual ice-coated hairs began to clack together like rhythmical castanets attuned to the motion of his body. It was snowing quite heavily in our faces now and it seemed to be approaching dusk, although I doubted if it were so on the land which I could now no longer see. I realized all the obvious things I should have considered earlier. That if the snow was blowing in our faces, the wind was off the land, and if it was off the land, it was blowing the ice pack back out to sea. That was probably one reason why the seam had opened. And also that the ice had only been "in" one night and had not had a chance to "set." I realized other things as well. That it was the time of the late afternoon when the tide was falling. That no one knew where we were. That I had said we were going to look at snares, which was not where we had gone at all. And I remembered now that I had received no answer even to that misinformation, so perhaps I had not even been heard. And also if there was drifting snow like this on land, our tracks would by now have been obliterated.

We came to a rough section of ice: huge slabs on their sides and others piled one on top of the other as if they were in some strange form of storage. It was no longer possible to ride the sleigh but as I stood up I lifted it and hung on to it as a means of holding on to the dog. The line usually attached to his collar had sunk with the vanished seal. My knees were stiff when I stood up; and deprived of the windbreak effect which the dog had provided, I felt the snow driving full into my face, particularly my eyes. It did not merely impede my vision, the way distant snow flurries might, but actually entered my eyes, causing them to water and freeze nearly shut. I was aware of the weight of ice on my eyelashes and could see them as they gradually lowered and became heavier. I did not remember ice like this when I got on, although I did not find that terribly surprising. I pressed the soles of my numbed feet firmly down upon it to try and feel if it was moving out, but it was impossible to tell because there was no fixed point of reference. Almost the sensation one gets on a conveyor belt at airports or on escalators; although you are standing still you recognize motion, but should you shut your eyes and be deprived of sight, even that recognition may become ambiguously uncertain.

The dog began to whine and to walk around me in circles, binding my legs with the traces of the harness as I continued to grasp the sleigh. Finally I decided to let him go as there seemed no way to hold him and there was nothing else to do. I unhitched the traces and doubled them up as best I could and tucked them under the backpad of his harness so they would not drag behind him and become snagged on any obstacles. I did not take off my mitts to do so as I was afraid I would not be able to get them back on. He vanished into the snow almost immediately.

The sleigh had been a gift from an uncle, so I hung on to it and carried it with both hands before me like an ineffectual shield against the wind and snow. I lowered my head as much as I could and turned it sideways so the wind would beat against my head instead of directly into my face. Sometimes I would turn and walk backwards for a few steps. Although I knew it was not the wisest thing to do, it seemed at times the only way to breathe. And then I began to feel the water sloshing about my feet.

Sometimes when the tides or currents ran heavily and the ice began to separate, the water that was beneath it would well up and wash over it almost as if it were re-flooding it. Sometimes you could see the hard ice clearly beneath the water but at other times a sort of floating slush was formed mingling with snow and "slob" ice which was not yet solid. It was thick and dense and soupy and it was impossible to see what lay beneath it. Experienced men on the ice sometimes carried a slender pole so they could test the consistency of the footing which might or might not lie before them, but I was obviously not one of them, although I had a momentary twinge for the pole I had used to dislodge the seal. Still, there was nothing to do but go forward.

When I went through, the first sensation was almost of relief and relaxation for the water initially made me feel much warmer than I had been on the surface. It was the most dangerous of false sensations for I knew my clothes were becoming heavier by the second. I clung to the sleigh somewhat as a raft and lunged forward with it in a kind of up-and-down swimming motion, hoping that it might strike some sort of solidity before my arms became so weighted and sodden that I could no longer lift them. I cried out then for the first time into the driving snow.

He came almost immediately, although I could see he was afraid and the slobbing slush was up to his knees. Still, he seemed to be on some kind of solid footing for he was not swimming. I splashed towards him and when almost there, desperately threw the sleigh before me and lunged for the edge of what seemed like his footing, but it only gave way as if my hands were closing on icy insubstantial porridge. He moved forward then, although I still could not tell if what supported him would be of any use to me. Finally I grasped the breast strap of his harness. He began to back up then, and as I said, he was tremendously strong. The harness began to slide forward on his shoulders but he continued to pull as I continued to grasp and then I could feel my elbows on what seemed like solid ice and I was able to hook them on the edge and draw myself, dripping and soaking, like another seal out of the black water and onto the whiteness of the slushy ice. Almost at once my clothes began to freeze. My elbows and knees began to creak when I bent them as if I were a robot from the realm of science fiction and then I could see myself clothed in transparent ice as if I had been coated with shellac or finished with clear varnish.

As the fall into the winter sea had at first seemed ironically warm, so now my garments of ice seemed a protection against the biting wind, but I knew it was a deceptive sensation and that I did not have much time before me. The dog faced into the wind and I followed him. This time he stayed in sight, and at times even turned back to wait for me. He was cautious but certain and gradually the slush disappeared, and although we were still in water, the ice was hard and clear beneath it. The frozen heaviness of my clothes began to weigh on me and I could feel myself, ironically, perspiring within my suit of icy armour. I was very tired, which I knew was another dangerous sensation. And then I saw the land. It was very close and a sudden surprise. Almost like coming upon a stalled and unexpected automobile in a highway's winter storm. It was only yards away, and although there was no longer any ice actually touching the shore, there were several pans of it floating in the region between. The dog jumped from one to the other and I followed him, still clutching the sleigh, and missing only the last pan which floated close to the rocky shore. The water came only to my waist and I was able to touch the bottom and splash noisily on land. We had been spared again for a future time and I was never to know whether he had reached the shore himself and come back or whether he had heard my call against the wind.

We began to run towards home and the land lightened and there were touches of evening sun. The wind still blew but no snow was falling. Yet when I looked back, the ice and the ocean were invisible in the swirling squalls. It was like looking at another far and distant country on the screen of a snowy television.

I became obsessed, now that I could afford the luxury, with not being found disobedient or considered a fool. The visitors' vehicles were still in the yard so I imagined most of the family to be in the parlour or living room, and I circled the house and entered through the kitchen, taking the dog with me. I was able to get upstairs unnoticed and get my clothes changed and when I came down I mingled with everybody and tried to appear as normal as I could. My own family was caught up with the visitors and only general comments came my way. The dog, who could not change his clothes, lay under the table with his head on his paws and he was also largely unnoticed. Later as the ice melted from his coat, a puddle formed around him, which I casually mopped up. Still later someone said, "I wonder where that dog has been, his coat is soaking wet." I was never to tell anyone of the afternoon's experience or that he had saved my life.

Two winters later I was sitting at a neighbour's kitchen table when I looked out the window and saw the dog as he was shot. He had followed my father and also me and had been sitting rather regally on a little hill beside the house and I suppose had presented an ideal target. But he had moved at just the right or wrong time and instead of killing him the high-powered bullet smashed into his shoulder. He jumped into the air and turned his snapping teeth upon the wound, trying to bite the cause of the pain he could not see. And then he turned towards home, unsteady but still strong on his three remaining legs. No doubt he felt, as we all do, that if he could get home he might be saved, but he did not make it, as we knew he could not, because of the amount of blood on the snow and the wavering pattern of his three-legged tracks. Yet he was, as I said, tremendously strong and he managed almost three-quarters of a mile. The house he sought must have been within his vision when he died for we could see it quite clearly when we came to his body by the roadside. His eyes were open and his tongue was clenched between his teeth and the little blood he had left dropped red and black on the winter snow. He was not to be saved for a future time anymore.

I learned later that my father had asked the neighbour to shoot him and that we had led him into a kind of ambush. Perhaps my father did so because the neighbour was younger and had a better gun or was a better shot. Perhaps because my father did not want to be involved. It was obvious he had not planned on things turning out so messy.

The dog had become increasingly powerful and protective, to the extent that people were afraid to come into the yard. And he had also bitten two of the neighbour's children and caused them to be frightened of passing our house on their journeys to and from school. And perhaps there was also the feeling in the community that he was getting more than his share of the breeding: that he travelled farther than other dogs on his nightly forays and that he fought off and injured the other smaller dogs who might compete with him for female favours. Perhaps there was fear that his dominance and undesirable characteristics did not bode well for future generations.

This has been the writing down of a memory triggered by the sight of a golden dog at play in the silent snow with my own excited children. After they came in and had their hot chocolate, the wind began to blow; and by the time I left for work, there was no evidence of their early-morning revels or any dog tracks leading to the chain-link fence. The "enclosed" dog looked impassively at me as I brushed the snow from the buried windshield. What does he know? he seemed to say.

The snow continues to drift and to persist as another uncertainty added to those we already have. Should we be forced to drive tonight, it will be a long, tough journey into the wind and the driving snow which is pounding across Ontario and Quebec and New Brunswick and against the granite coast of Nova Scotia. Should we be drawn by death, we might well meet our own. Still, it is only because I am alive that I can even consider such possibilities. Had I not been saved by the golden dog, I would not have these tight concerns or children playing in the snow or of course these memories. It is because of him that I have been able to come this far in time.

It is too bad that I could not have saved him as well and my feelings did him little good as I looked upon his bloodied body there beside the road. It was too late and out of my control and even if I had known the possibilities of the future it would not have been easy.

He was with us only for a while and brought his own changes, and yet he still persists. He persists in my memory and in my life and he persists physically as well. He is there in this winter storm. There in the golden-grey dogs with their black-tipped ears and tails, sleeping in the stables or in the lees of woodpiles or under porches or curled beside the houses which face towards the sea.

The Pain of the Indian by Sarain Stump, 1973, acrylic on split sheepskin with mounte[d]
wooden mask.

An Afternoon in Bright Sunlight

SHIRLEY BRUISED HEAD 1987

Long before the coming of white explorers and settlers, what is now known as Canada was home to the First Nations—Cree, Huron, Ojibwa, Haida and many others. This tale is by a member of the Blackfoot Nation, whose people once roamed freely as hunters across the Great Plains including what is now called Alberta. In this disturbing and mysterious tale, Shirley Bruised Head uses all her poetic skill to create an encounter between two ways of life, one immensely old and one relatively new. She also follows the great tradition of First Nation storytelling, introducing her tale, setting up a predicament—and leaving you, the reader, to create its ending.

Ayissomaawa ...

The Porcupine Hills look soft and brown as we stand gazing out over sunburnt prairie grass.

"Come on, guys. Let's go for a ride," says Hank.

Hank is boss. At least he thinks he is. He is a year older than Anne and me and is the only boy in the family. We let him get away with it, sometimes.

Anne agrees with him. She always agrees with him, especially when we have nothing to do. "We'll ask Mom to make some sandwiches."

"Good idea. Tell her we're going to hunt arrowheads."

Hank decides Anne will ride Brownie, a twelve-year-old bay gelding, same age as Hank. He chooses Hoss for me. Hank says, "Hoss needs some kinks worked out, and this is as good a day as any." He chooses Buck, because Buck is his horse and Buck understands him.

Mom packs enough food to last a week, and, as we make our way back to the corral, she comes to the door and yells, "Don't go too far into the coulee, and watch out for rattlesnakes." She mangles a dish-towel. "Keep an eye open for that bear Jerry saw last week. He says he spotted it down by the old school and later saw it moving toward the hills." She shakes out the towel and waves it. "Get home before dark." She smiles. "Have a good time."

"All right," I yell. "We'll be careful."

"Don't let her worry you." Anne picks up the sack. "There are no rattlesnakes in the coulee, and you know Jerry lies a lot."

"I know Jerry lies. I'm not worried."

Hank has the horses saddled and ready to go. He takes the sack and ties it to the back of his saddle.

A wide streak of dust rises, billows out, and kind of hangs in the air. "There's Dad," says Hank. He pats Buck's neck.

Mom doesn't look too pleased. The dust mushrooms. We hear Dad's loud laughing voice, "Hello Dawlink!" Mom takes a swipe at him with her dish-towel. "I brought company," he says.

"Isn't that old Sam?" says Hank.

Mom shakes hands with Sam; her voice carries on the breeze. "Come in. I'll make you something to eat."

Everybody treats Sam with respect. I remember walking in front of him one time, and, boy, did I ever get it from Dad. I stay out of his way now.

Hank is all excited. "There's Les!"

Les comes running. We all think Les is the greatest. Dad picks him up whenever he needs help. He trains horses for Dad. He trained Hoss, and helps out during calving season. He travels with Dad, and, sometimes, he even drives. He seems older than fourteen.

"Hey, Les," says Hank. "You can ride Hoss."

"Where you going?" Les lengthens the stirrups. "Hunting arrowheads."

Anne and I stand there listening. They ignore us. They always ignore us.

"Hey! You kids!" shouts Dad from the house. Hank shoves me and Anne up on Brownie, and we take off. We can hear Dad shouting. We reach the coulee, and Hank reins in. Les looks at him.

"Your dad was calling.'

"I know."

"You guys are in trouble."

"He wants us to stay home."

"Well," says Les. "We might as well keep going now. We'll catch heck for one thing or another."

"I know, but maybe if we stay out late, he'll cool off."

"Yeah, he'll get worried," says Anne.

"Yeah, he'll just have more to get mad about," I say.

They just look at me.

We wander into the coulees, stopping every now and then to pick cactus berries. They are green and plump, the size of grapes. Their juice is sweet and sticky. They are easy to find in the short grass, and we go from patch to patch

As we near an outcropping of rock, Anne says, "Mom said to watch out for rattlesnakes."

"Don't be silly. Everybody knows there are no rattlesnakes in these coulees. Right, Hank?"

Hank and I agree.

"Well, how about that bear Jerry saw?" says Anne.

"Jerry didn't see no bear," laughs Les.

"Are you sure?" Hank licks his lips whenever he's worried. He does it now.

"Sure I'm sure. There hasn't been a bear in these coulees for years."

"Well, a bear could have come down from the hills."

"Look," says Les, "there are no bears in the coulee."

That settles the bear question. We stay away from the rocks. Everybody knows that snakes sun themselves on rocks. None of us likes snakes, especially Hank and Anne.

Hank licks his lips. "Jerry lies a lot."

"You still worried?" says Les.

"I just remembered Dad said he saw something out here."

"I remember, too," says Anne eagerly. "It was the day before Jerry came to visit."

"It was after," I say.

"It was before," says Hank.

Anne smiles at me. "I told you," she says.

"Come to think of it," says Les, "just before we came out, we were at the pool hall in town. Your dad, Sam, and some other men were talking about seeing something out here."

"What did they see?"

"Do you know anything about Sam?"

"Yeah. He's old, and he lives by the school," says Hank.

"You're not supposed to walk in front of him," I say. "Did you know that?"

Anne wants to know more. "What about him?"

Les looks at Hank. "Do you know why he lives there?'

"No."

"He guards the coulees."

We look at Les. He looks back. He isn't smiling. His eyes sweep over us. Then he turns and carefully guides Hoss around a clump of brittle reeds down onto a dry creek bed.

"What do you mean, he guards the coulees?"

"Just that."

"Why should he guard the coulees?" Les has me curious, too.

"Oh," says Les, "there's things out here."

"What kind of things?"

"Animals . . . other things that live in the coulee."

"You've got to be kidding. Only animals live in the coulee." Hank shakes his head and laughs.

"What kind of things?" I insist.

"You don't have to know," Hank cuts in. "What did old Sam have to say?"

In a matter-of-fact tone, Les says, "He thinks a wolverine may have moved in."

"A wolverine? No kidding!" Hank's eyes light up. He moves closer to Les. "Maybe we should forget about arrowheads and go hunting."

"I don't think so."

"But, I've never seen a wolverine. It would be fun."

"We better wait until Sam figures out what to do."

"What does Sam have to do with anything?"

"Sam knows a lot. He says they're dangerous."

I break in—"That's what Emma said."

"Yeah? What did Emma have to say?"

"You're not supposed to listen to Emma," says Anne.

"Well, she says they're dangerous and evil, too."

"Forget about Emma," Hank says, licking his lips. "She's a crazy old lady. Just how dangerous are wolverines?"

"Well, you know that bear?" says Les.

"Yeah?"

"Well, wolverines hunt the hunter."

Hank looks over his shoulder. Anne and I smile.

It is hot. Horse tails switch lazily at slow-moving flies. Saddle leather squeaks. Hooves thud dully on dry grass. An occasional sharp crack echoes down the coulee.

She stands listening to the children's voices. An outcropping of rock hides her den. Inside, it is cool and dry.

Ayissomaawaawa . . . I must be careful, I waited long. Need to grow. Strong. Strong. Strong as when I was young. It was good. Our power was strong

Must be careful. Haste betrays. I must wait. Come, boy. Come alone. Do not fear. There is nothing to fear.

"Hank!" Anne yells. "Look at the chokecherries!"

Low chokecherry bushes grow halfway up to the side of the coulee. Their branches hang with thick clusters of black cherries.

"Let's pick some for Mom," I say.

Hank dismounts. "Good idea, Girlie. Here, you hold the horses."

"Why do I always have to hold the horses?"

"Because I tell you to."

I look down at him. "We can't pick berries, anyway."

"Why not?"

"We have nothing to put them in."

"We can put them in the lunch sack," says Anne.

"Good idea," says Hank. "We can tie the horses up down by those bushes."

I must wait. Cannot hurry. Wait. Not strong. Stronger must I get. Soon. Soon. So close.

The bushes are low and evenly spaced. They look as if they were planted by someone. Anne and I fill our hats and empty the berries into the sack. We begin filling our hats again, when Anne spots some raspberries growing near the outcropping of rock.

"Come on, Hank. Let's get some of them, too."

"I'm not going over there."

Anne looks at me. I shake my head.

"Just look at them!"

"Go and get them, then," says Les.

"Yeah." Hank and I agree.

"I don't know." Anne looks at the rocks.

"Nobody's stopping you," says Les.

"There might be snakes."

"Snakes won't kill you. These snakes are just ordinary snakes," says Les.

"Then you go and get them."

"I don't like raspberries."

Ayissomaawa . . . Patience. Must have patience. Soon I will have them. I must have them. Must be careful. Not move. Too soon. Wait. Time. Old woman. Now old woman. Do not frighten.

"Let's go, then. You girls wait for us here. Okay?"

"Why do we have to wait?"

Hank is real nasty. "All right. If you want to walk down, I'm not stopping you."

"I'm not going anyplace." Anne drops to the ground. "You guys can get the horses."

Hank and Les run down the coulee.

"Do you smell something funny?" says Anne.

"Yeah, it smells like sage."

"No. Sage doesn't smell like that."

"Maybe it's dry mint."

"No. Mint doesn't smell like that, either."

"Maybe it's a snake den. Snakes like rocks, you know."

"No. It isn't snakes."

"How do you know?"

"I know," says Anne. "Now quit. You're giving me a headache."

We sit there. The sun is beating down. It is quiet. Flies drone. I feel sleepy. The sun is warm on my back.

Ayissomaawa . . .

"Anne! Girlie! Get over here."

Les and Hank have the horses. They wait while we bring the sack of berries.

"Come on. Hurry up!"

"I don't feel so good, Hank," says Anne. "I have a headache."

"Me, too."

Hank and Les look at each other. "So do we."

"Maybe we should just go home."

"We can't let a stupid headache stop us from hunting for arrowheads."

Anne and me stand there, looking at Hank. Nobody says anything. Hank looks at us. "Just around the bend is where we found them last time."

"I wonder if there are any left," says Les.

"There should be plenty."

"What happened to the other ones we found?"

"Mom still has them. She takes them out every once in a while."

Ayissomaawa ... Horses. Horses know us. Must be careful.

"Are we going to hunt arrowheads or stand around here all day?" I say.

"We're going. Now get on that horse."

Hank lifts Anne and me up on Brownie and ties the sack to his saddle. "Ready to go?"

"Yeah."

The horses walk sideways. Their ears flick back and forth. Their eyes roll, and they jerk their heads up and down. We don't go very far.

"What's that smell?"

"Smells like sage to me."

"No, it doesn't." Anne is emphatic. I agree with her.

"Well, it doesn't smell half bad. It sure is strange, though. Wonder what's causing it." Les looks around.

"What's that?" Anne points to the rocks. I try to see over her shoulder.

"Where?"

"Over there. See?"

"It's just a shadow."

"There's something there," says Anne.

The horses balk. Hoss backs into Brownie.

"Let's go see. Let's find out what it is. Come on, Hank."

Hank licks his lips. "Do you think we should?"

We look at him.

"Well, the horses don't want to go."

Les stands up in his stirrups to get a better view. A surprised look crosses his face.

"It's an old woman."

Brownie whirls. Takes off down the side of the coulee. Anne and I hold on tight. I didn't know Brownie had that much speed. As we hit the bottom of the coulee, I see two riders loom up in front of us. Brownie stumbles, and both of us fall.

"Are you hurt?" Dad sounds worried.

"No," I say, and he pulls me off Anne.

"Anne, Anne, you all right?"

Anne lies there, trying to catch her breath. I look up and see Sam.

"Anne, you all right?"

"Yeah, Dad. I'm okay." Anne lies back and starts to cry.

Before Hank and Les can slide to a stop, Dad is already yelling. "How many times have I told you not to run the horses like that?"

"We didn't do nothing." Hank points back to the rocks. "The horses . . . they just took off when they saw that old lady in the coulee."

"What are you talking about?"

"An old woman . . . in the coulee." Hank looks at Les.

"She spooked the horses," says Les.

Dad looks back and forth, eyeing each of us. He knows we wouldn't dare lie to him.

"Did you see her?"

"We didn't get a good look," says Les.

Dad looks at us and then at Sam.

"It was near those rocks," says Hank.

"Yeah, and it smelled kinda like sage," says Les.

"You kids get home right now," says Dad. He shoves me and Anne back up on Brownie. "Get going! Stay there till I get back."

We know an order when we hear one.

Too late. Must move. Always moving. He'll come. Tired. Tired. He has power. He will come. No more.

Dad stands at the mouth of the coulee holding the two horses. Sam walks into the coulee.

Saturday Climbing

W. D. VALGARDSON 1982

It is not only in tourist brochures that Canada is often called the land of the great outdoors, for its own people delight in its space and freedom — from camping beside one of its great lakes, to hunting in its northern forests or meeting the challenges of its great mountains. What do people find when they leave their safe, urban lives for a little while? Here, the author explores what happens when a father and his daughter go climbing and meet in some ways almost as strangers.

Sixty feet up the cliff, the toe of his climbing boot resting on a ledge no wider than a dime, two fingers curled around a nubbin of rock, Barry was suddenly afraid that he would fall. "Rope," he called.

At the foot of the cliff, his daughter let out the golden line of rope that joined them. As Barry felt the rope go slack, he raised his right knee and pressed his toe into a shallow depression. Grunting with the strain, he stood up on his right leg, then paused, uncertain of his next move.

The cliff had proven to be deceptive. The conglomerate, with its rough, gravel-like surface, had looked easy. Close to the base, there were large handholds, so that at first the climbing was little more difficult than walking up stairs. Then, unexpectedly, the surfaces smoothed; the places where he could get a secure hold were spread farther and farther apart. At the same time, the numerous cracks dwindled until there was no place to set any protection. Unable to go back because of his pride, he had continued on until he now found himself dangerously far above his last piton. If he fell, he would drop twenty-five feet to the piton, then twenty-five feet past it before his rope came taut and held him. There was, because of the elasticity of the rope, a chance that he would ground out.

The thought flitted through his mind that it would be like falling from the top of a six-storey building. Tensing his fingers, he straightened his elbow and leaned back from the rock so that he could search for his next hold. Above him, there was a half-inch ledge. He reached up, got a good grip, then lifted his left leg higher than he had ever imagined he could and set his foot on a rough patch that would provide the necessary friction to hold his weight.

He had been scared many times but never like this. Never before had he

The Wall by Nigel Roe, No. 8 Random Pattern, 1981, graphite, pencil and coloured pencil on paper.

been this close to paralysis, to a sensation of letting go so that the tension and the fear would be over. The way he felt, he imagined, was the way a wounded animal felt when it finally gave up fleeing and allowed itself to be killed.

Six inches from his left hand there was a vertical crack that seemed hardly wider than a fingernail. Cautiously, he explored it with his fingers. Just within his reach it widened slightly. He ran his hand over his rack and unsnapped the smallest chock nut. He forced the aluminium wedge deep into the crack. From the wedge there hung a wire loop and from that a carabiner. Catching hold of the rope tied to his harness, he lifted it up, forced open the spring-loaded gate of the carabiner and fitted the rope into the aluminium oval.

Once the gate snapped shut, he sighed with relief. The chock nut, the wire loop, the carabiner, the rope, fragile as they looked, would hold ten times his weight. If he wanted to, he could let go and simply hang in space.

"You all right?" his daughter called. "Yeah," he lied. "Just resting."

His voice sounded faint and breathy. He was glad she could not see his momentary weakness. He could not control the trembling of his legs. The muscle of his right arm jerked spasmodically. Ever since his wife had left him, he had tried to compensate by providing unhesitating leadership for his daughter. He did his best to keep life simple and uncomplicated. It was, he thought, the way to provide security.

He glanced down. Among the scattered grey boulders, Moira's red hair gleamed like a burnished cap.

"You're doing fine," she hollered. The crosscurrents of air that played over the cliff face blurred her voice, making it seem farther away than it really was. To hear what she said, he had to strain toward the sound. "You've got another twenty feet to a big ledge. You can do it easy."

He was grateful for her confidence. Before they had started climbing, there had crept into his daughter's voice a constant note of disparagement and disappointment. The times he had managed to overcome his own insecurity and had asked her what was the matter, she had turned her back on him, answering, "Nothing," with a tightly controlled voice.

Bewildered, he had sought the advice of women at work who had teenage daughters. They had been no help. Behind their competent, efficient professional selves, they too, he realized, were just as confused as he was. In desperation, he had gone so far as to pose the question of the relationship of fathers and daughters to his class. He had not been prepared for the reaction he got. From every corner of the room came cries of bitter disappointment and resentment.

As he had left the classroom, one student had called to him. He had stopped to wait for her. She had frizzy dark hair, wore long dresses that might have come from a western movie set, a rainbow assortment of beads, and a nose ring. She always talked as if she was thinking in some exotic language and was translating it badly. She was the only student he'd ever had who insisted on analyzing *War and Peace* by consulting the *I Ching*.

"The caged bird proves nothing but the power of the captor," she had intoned.

For a moment, he suffered vertigo, and the cliff seemed to sway as if in an earthquake. He pressed his forehead to the cool stone and shut his eyes. Inside his flesh, his bones trembled.

Taking up rock-climbing had been an act of desperation. All the past activities Moira and he had done together — going to foreign films, visiting Seattle, beachcombing — she dismissed with a contemptuous shrug of her shoulders. At one time, they had played chess nearly every day. Lately, she pretended she had never seen the game. When he had noticed an advertisement for rock-climbing, he remembered that she had spoken admiringly of classmates who had hiked the West Coast Trail. He had registered them and paid their fees. Then he informed her.

He hoped she would be pleased. Instead, she was incensed that he had committed her to something without her consent. He knew she was right to be angry but he was too frantic to care. Over the previous month, she had come home late a number of times. Each time, the sweet-sour smell of marijuana clung to her, and her pupils seemed unnaturally large. He had not dared to accuse her of smoking dope. If he was wrong, she would never forgive him for being unjust. Being right frightened him even more. If she said, "That's right, I'm smoking dope, six joints a day, and sniffing coke and participating in orgies," he didn't know what he would do. Ranting and raving had ceased to work. Reasoning with her had no effect. He felt utterly helpless.

By emphasizing that the money was spent and there was no refund, he won the argument over rock-climbing. However, he took the car to the first class while she took her bike. She went prepared to sneer at everything, but once she saw her classmates, her attitude changed.

Instead of Moira being isolated by her youth, Barry was isolated because of his age. Of the fifteen members, eleven were under twenty. The instructor still didn't need to shave more than once a week.

By the time the three hours were over and he realized that rock-climbing wasn't going to be rough hiking, it was too late to back out. There were only three girls in the class. In return for the attention of one-third of the young men, Moira was prepared to scale the Himalayas.

Barry began with an attitude that was typical of someone raised on the Prairies. Anything over three feet was a substantial elevation. During the second class, he was expected to climb vertical cliffs. He gave some thought to dropping out of the class but realized that, after the fuss he had made about the fees, he would look like a dreadful hypocrite.

Gradually, as a dozen Saturdays passed, what had seemed impossible was reduced to the merely difficult. Cliffs that had looked flat and smooth as polished marble became a series of problems and solutions. The names of the unfamiliar equipment became a part of his vocabulary. Young men in climbing boots frequented his backyard and kitchen. To his relief, Moira accepted him enough to spend an occasional hour practising knot-tying with him.

This weekend there had been no class. In an attempt to heal a rift caused by an argument over her going away to college — she was two years ahead of herself in school, and therefore, in spite of being in grade 12 was only 16 — he had offered to go climbing with her. To his surprise, she'd accepted.

"Climbing," he called.

"Climb on," Moira answered.

He stepped up, away from the safety of his perch. His life, he realized was in her hands. If he fell, she was his protection.

The thought of giving her so much responsibility was like the prick of a thorn. In all other things, he had been trying to keep her from rushing headlong into taking on too much responsibility at once. The result had been a long series of disagreements. She did not have the decency to let one dispute finish before she began another. Sometimes three or four overlapped.

On Fridays, when he went to the faculty club, he ordered double brandies and brooded over whether he shouldn't have insisted on Sunday school in a good fundamentalist church all the past years. His colleagues, the majority of whom were the epitome of liberal tolerance about most things, when they talked about their teenage children reverted to wistful fantasies about convents and boarding schools in inaccessible locations.

The weekend past, Moira had wanted to go to an all-night party with a boy he just vaguely recognized as having drifted through the house two or three times. Barry was dumbfounded. At the same age, he'd had to have his girlfriends in before midnight. If he had kept a girl out all night, her father would have met them with a shotgun.

"Good girls," he said, quoting something he'd heard in adolescence, "don't stay out all night."

"Good fathers," she shot back, "don't think the worst of their daughters."

That afternoon was filled with slamming doors, weeping and raised voices. He found himself fighting so hard against her staying out all night that he compromised on three o'clock and afterward, when he had calmed down, wondered how it had happened. He had been determined to start with a deadline of midnight and let himself be persuaded to accept one o'clock. Although Moira claimed not to remember the chess moves, he had the distinct feeling that he'd been checkmated.

The final blow had been her insistence on going away to college. They had the money, he admitted. It just wasn't sensible, at sixteen, to travel 2,000 miles to attend a school when the local university was every bit as good, even if it did have him on the faculty. He suspected the choice had more to do with her all-night-party boy than with academic excellence.

Now, as he worked his way up toward the large ledge where he was to set up a belay station, it was as if Barry were in danger of being pulled backwards by the sheer weight of his memories. It was with a sense of relief that he heaved himself onto the ledge. He paused to catch his breath, then anchored himself to a boulder.

"On belay," he shouted down, giving Moira the signal that he was ready.

His daughter, eighty feet below, seemed so small that Barry felt he could lift her into his arms. She looked no larger than she had been when, at three, she had eaten a bottle of aspirin. He had scooped her up and run with her four blocks to the hospital. After that desperate race and the struggle to hold her down — it had taken both him and a nurse to control her flailing limbs while the doctor had pumped her stomach — he was acutely aware of how tenuous her life was, of how much he would suffer if he lost her. For a long time afterward, he thought of her as being intricately constructed of fragile paper.

"Climbing," Moira answered.

"Climb on," he shouted.

From time to time, she paused to pull loose the chock nuts and pitons her father had left behind. These, since they would be needed later, she clipped to a sling that hung over her shoulder. Once, when she deviated from the route her father had taken, she became stuck at an overhang. Not having dealt with the obstacle himself, Barry could not help and had to leave her to find her own solution.

The climb seemed agonizingly slow, as if it would never be completed. Then, when it was over, and his daughter, grinning, breathless, was climbing over the edge, it was as if hardly any time had passed.

They sat side by side, sipping orange juice, their feet dangling in space.

"I thought you were in trouble," Moira said.

"I thought you were too," he replied, matching his weakness with hers. Then, ashamed, he admitted, "I gripped."

Moira twisted about. Her red hair was snugged at the back with a rubber band. Being outside had sprinkled her nose with light freckles.

She studied the cliff face. It rose another hundred feet. There was a crack that ran more than halfway, then a small series of outcrops. He tried to see the route they should take, but the last ten or fifteen feet seemed impossible.

"I'd come home for Christmas," she said in a rush, "and classes are out in April. It's not as if it was such a long time to be away."

She had caught him unawares, and none of his carefully prepared arguments were at hand.

"It's just so unexpected," was all that he could manage.

"I've got to leave sometime."

The house will be so empty, he wanted to say. How will I get used to being alone? It is as if you lost your first tooth only last year. As if I took you to kindergarten six months ago. You're barely rid of your braces.

She lifted her index finger and rubbed the side of her nose. She had done it as long as he could remember. It was her signal that she was going to impart a confidence or confess a wrongdoing—that she liked some boy in her class, that she had got a detention or spent all her allowance before the end of the week and needed more money.

"I'm not innocent, you know."

He wondered what she meant by that but was afraid to ask.

"I mean," she continued, "Vic Hi's a big school. You hear a lot. Everybody's on the Pill. The dope's there if you want it. There's lots of opportunity."

He was tempted to let loose his anxiety in a lecture, but the memory of the frizzy-haired student in his class stopped him. She had stood on one foot all the time they were talking, the sole of her left sandal pressed to her right knee. She had passed her hand before his face in an affected arc. He'd heard her father was a prominent lawyer in the East but found it hard to believe.

She had talked in aphorisms and riddles, then a silence had fallen between them. He'd wondered why she had bothered to call after him, what she had really wanted to say. He had left her but after a few steps, glanced back. She had given up her storklike stance and was standing with feet together, shoulders slumped, her face slack beneath her gaudy makeup. For the first time, he had seen how much younger she was than he had thought. If he had not known better, he'd have said she was a lost child.

Just then, she had seen him watching her. Immediately, she had drawn up her shoulders, flung back her head, given an exaggerated sway of her hips and pranced away. That had been the last time he'd seen her. She had never come back to his class, and one day a yellow drop-slip with her name on it had appeared in his mailbox.

"I want to lead this pitch," Moira said.

Barry was startled. She had never led. Always before she'd been second or third on a rope.

"I was thinking of rappelling down," he answered. "I can't see a clear route up."

"There," she said. "There and there and there." She jabbed her fingertip at a series of holds.

"But where would you set your protection?"

Her hand wove a series of stitches in the air. "There. Up there. To the side. Back across. Up about six feet."

His fear for her was not without reason. The climbing, after seeming so dangerous at first, had begun to lose its aura of hazard. They all fell from time to time, but their ropes kept them from suffering more than bruised knees and elbows. Then, one of the climbers who was leading had ignored instructions, and, overconfident, had put in only one piece of protection. He placed it improperly, and when he slipped and fell, his weight jerked it loose. For a moment, no one had been able to move, then those who were not belaying or climbing had run toward the boy who lay sprawled on his back. Bright red blood seeped from his nose and ear.

"Jackets," Barry had demanded. Red Cross training that he'd not thought about in years came back with an intense clarity. "Every piece of clothing you can spare. We mustn't let him get cold."

They all had moved automatically, clumsily, unable to think. Having done as he instructed, they all stood stupefied. Their faces were shocked white beneath their tans.

He sent two of the students racing down the hill for help.

For an hour, they huddled in a ragged circle around the boy whose hair was paler than the sun-drenched grass and whose skin might have been moulded from wax. He slipped in and out of consciousness. Each time his eyes shut, they all tensed, afraid that he had died. But then, he would groan or let out his breath harshly, and the moment would pass. Someone, Barry had not noticed who, had started collecting gear. One, and then another, began to pack. They moved slowly, silently, as if any noise would disturb the delicate balance between life and death.

Grounded out. That was what they called it. Because his safety had not been properly set, he had grounded out. Barry remembered that the air force had been like that too. Pilots never failed. They washed out. They never died. They bought it. *Grounded out.* The semantics covered up the fear.

Now, for a moment, it was as if, once again, he could hear the sharp startled cry; see the backward arc, the body, falling without grace or beauty, the rope writhing and twisting, the red-shirted boy settling in a cloud of unexpected dust.

"Ron," Barry protested, surprising himself at remembering the boy's name.

"Do you think I'd be so careless?"

It was asked in a tone that allowed no argument.

Stiffly, he stood up and tested his belay.

Don't climb, he thought, *it's too dangerous. Let us go back the way we came and find somewhere that'll always be safe.* But even as he thought it, he knew that it was impossible.

Once again, it was as if he were standing before the frizzy-haired girl, watching her long green nails sweep slowly before his face. At the time, he had not wanted to understand. "The world seeks balance," she'd said. "Extremism begets extremism."

"On belay," he said.

"Climbing," Moira replied.

His daughter, easily, with the supreme confidence of youth, grasped a handhold and pulled herself onto a flake. Smoothly, she worked her way up one side of the crack, straddled it and crossed over.

Below her, her father, ever watchful, full of fear, smoothly payed out the rope, determined to give her all the slack she needed while, at the same time, keeping his hands tensed, ready to lock shut, ready to absorb the shock of any fall.

Townscapes

An Ounce of Cure

ALICE MUNRO 1968

The delights and agonies of growing up are felt with equal intensity wherever someone lives. How powerful can these first experiences be—the first time in love, the first heartbreak, the first time you turn to an adult's remedy for your pain? Finding out can have unfortunate consequences anywhere—including Canada!

My parents didn't drink. They weren't rabid about it, and in fact I remember that when I signed the pledge in grade seven, with the rest of that superbly if impermanently indoctrinated class, my mother said, "It's just nonsense and fanaticism, children of that age." My father would drink a beer on a hot day, but my mother did not join him, and—whether accidentally or symbolically—this drink was always consumed *outside* the house. Most of the people we knew were the same way, in the small town where we lived. I ought not to say that it was this which got me into difficulties, because the difficulties I got into were a faithful expression of my own incommodious nature—the same nature that caused my mother to look at me, on any occasion which traditionally calls for feelings of pride and maternal accomplishment (my departure for my first formal dance, I mean, or my hellbent preparations for a descent on college) with an expression of brooding and fascinated despair, as if she could not possibly expect, did not ask, that it should go with me as it did with other girls; the dreamed-of spoils of daughters—orchids, nice boys, diamond rings—would be borne home in due course by the daughters of her friends, but not by me; all she could do was hope for a lesser rather than a greater disaster—an elopement, say, with a boy who could never earn his living, rather than an abduction into the White Slave trade.

But ignorance, my mother said, ignorance, or innocence if you like, is not always such a fine thing as people think and I am not sure it may not be dangerous for a girl like you; then she emphasized her point, as she had a habit of doing, with some quotation which had an innocent pomposity and odour of mothballs. I didn't even wince at it, knowing full well how it must have worked wonders with Mr. Berryman.

The evening I baby-sat for the Berrymans must have been in April. I had

Modern Times by Nathan Petroff, 1937, watercolour over graphite on wove paper.

been in love all year, or at least since the first week in September, when a boy named Martin Collingwood had given me a surprised, appreciative, and rather ominously complacent smile in the school assembly. I never knew what surprised him; I was not looking like anybody but me; I had an old blouse on and my home-permanent had turned out badly. A few weeks after that he took me out for the first time, and kissed me on the dark side of the porch—also, I ought to say, on the mouth; I am sure it was the first time anybody had ever kissed me effectively, and I know that I did not wash my face that night or the next morning, in order to keep the imprint of those kisses intact. (I showed the most painful banality in the conduct of this whole affair, as you will see.) Two months, and a few amatory stages later, he dropped me. He had fallen for the girl who played opposite him in the Christmas production of *Pride and Prejudice*.

I said I was not going to have anything to do with that play, and I got another girl to work on Makeup in my place, but of course I went to it after all, and sat down in front with my girl friend Joyce, who pressed my hand when I was overcome with pain and delight at the sight of Mr. Darcy in the white breeches, silk waistcoat, and sideburns. It was surely seeing Martin as Darcy that did for me; every girl is in love with Darcy anyway, and the part gave Martin an arrogance and male splendour in my eyes which made it impossible to remember that he was simply a high-school senior, passably good-looking and of medium intelligence (and with a reputation slightly tainted, at that, by such preferences as the Drama Club and the Cadet Band), who happened to be the first boy, the first really presentable boy, to take an interest in me. In the last act they gave him a chance to embrace Elizabeth (Mary Bishop, with a sallow complexion and no figure, but big vivacious eyes) and during this realistic encounter I dug my nails bitterly into Joyce's sympathetic palm.

That night was the beginning of months of real, if more or less self-inflicted, misery for me. Why is it a temptation to refer to this sort of thing lightly, with irony, with amazement even, at finding oneself involved with such preposterous emotions in the unaccountable past? That is what we are apt to do, speaking of love; with adolescent love, of course, it's practically obligatory; you would think we sat around, dull afternoons, amusing ourselves with these tidbit recollections of pain. But it really doesn't make me feel very gay—worse still, it doesn't really surprise me—to remember all the stupid, sad, half-ashamed things I did, that people in love always do. I hung around the places where he might be seen, and then pretended not to see him; I made absurdly roundabout approaches, in conversation, to the bitter pleasure of casually mentioning his name. I daydreamed endlessly; in fact if you want to put it mathematically, I spent perhaps ten times as many hours thinking about Martin Collingwood—yes, pining and weeping for him—as I ever spent with him; the idea of him dominated my mind relentlessly and, after a while, against my will. For if at first I had dramatized my feelings, the time came when I would have been glad to escape them; my well-worn daydreams had become depressing and not even temporarily consoling. As I worked my math problems I would torture myself, quite mechanically and helplessly with an exact recollection of Martin kissing my throat. I had an exact recollection of *everything*. One night I had an impulse to swallow all the aspirins in the bathroom cabinet, but stopped after I had taken six.

My mother noticed that something was wrong and got me some iron pills. She said, "Are you sure everything is going all right at school?" *School!* When I told her that Martin and I had broken up, all she said was, "Well so much the better for that. I never saw a boy so stuck on himself." "Martin has enough conceit to sink a battleship," I said morosely and went upstairs and cried.

The night I went to the Berrymans' was a Saturday night. I baby-sat for them quite often on Saturday nights because they liked to drive over to Baileyville, a much bigger, livelier town about twenty miles away, and perhaps have supper and go to a show. They had been living in our town only two or three years—Mr. Berryman had been brought in as plant manager of the new door-factory—and they remained, I suppose by choice, on the fringes of its society; most of their friends were youngish couples like themselves, born in other places, who lived in new ranch-style houses on a hill outside town where we used to go tobogganing. This Saturday night they had two other couples in for drinks before they all drove over to Baileyville for the opening of a new supper-club; they were all rather festive. I sat in the kitchen and pretended to do Latin. Last night had been the Spring Dance at the High School. I had not gone, since the only boy who had asked me was Millerd Crompton, who asked so many girls that he was suspected of working his way through the whole class alphabetically. But the dance was held in the Armouries, which was only half a block away from our house; I had been able to see the boys in dark suits, the girls in long pale formals under their coats, passing gravely under the street lights, stepping around the last patches of snow. I could even hear the music and I have not forgotten to this day that they played "Ballerina", and—oh, song of my aching heart—"Slow Boat to China". Joyce had phoned me up this morning and told me in her hushed way (we might have been discussing an incurable disease I had) that yes, M.C. *had* been there with M.B., and she had on a formal that must have been made out of somebody's old lace tablecloth, it just *hung*.

When the Berrymans and their friends had gone I went into the living room and read a magazine. I was mortally depressed. The big softly lit room, with its green and leaf-brown colours, made an uncluttered setting for the development of the emotions, such as you would get on a stage. At home the life of the emotions went on all right, but it always seemed to get buried under the piles of mending to be done, the ironing, the children's jigsaw puzzles and rock collections. It was the sort of house where people were always colliding with one another on the stairs and listening to hockey games and Superman on the radio.

I got up and found the Berrymans' "Danse Macabre" and put it on the record player and turned out the living-room lights. The curtains were only partly drawn. A street light shone obliquely on the windowpane, making a rectangle of thin dusty gold, in which the shadows of bare branches moved, caught in the huge sweet winds of spring. It was a mild black night when the last snow was melting. A year ago all this—the music, the wind and darkness, the shadows of the branches—would have given me tremendous happiness; when they did not do so now, but only called up tediously familiar, somehow humiliatingly personal thoughts, I gave up my soul for dead and walked into the kitchen and decided to get drunk.

No, it was not like that. I walked into the kitchen to look for a Coke or something in the refrigerator, and there on the front of the counter were three tall beautiful bottles, all about half full of gold. But even after I had looked at them and lifted them to feel their weight, I had not decided to get drunk; I had decided to have a drink.

Now here is where my ignorance, my disastrous innocence, comes in. It is true that I had seen the Berrymans and their friends drinking their highballs as casually as I would drink a Coke, but I did not apply this attitude to myself. No; I thought of hard liquor as something to be taken in extremities and relied upon for extravagant results, one way or another. My approach could not have been less casual if I had been the Little Mermaid drinking the witch's crystal potion. Gravely, with a glance at my set face in the black window above the sink, I poured a little whisky from each of the bottles (I think now there were two brands of rye and an expensive Scotch) until I had my glass full. For I had never in my life seen anyone pour a drink and I had no idea that people frequently diluted their liquor with water, soda, et cetera, and I had seen that the glasses the Berrymans' guests were holding when I came through the living room were nearly full.

I drank it off as quickly as possible. I set the glass down and stood looking at my face in the window, half expecting to see it altered. My throat was burning, but I felt nothing else. It was very disappointing, when I had worked myself up to it. But I was not going to let it go at that. I poured another full glass, then filled each of the bottles with water to approximately the level I had seen when I came in. I drank the second glass only a little more slowly than the first. I put the empty glass down on the counter with care, perhaps feeling in my head a rustle of things to come, and went and sat down on a chair in the living room. I reached up and turned on a floor lamp beside the chair, and the room jumped on me.

When I say that I was expecting extravagant results I do not mean that I was expecting this. I had thought of some sweeping emotional change, an upsurge of gaiety and irresponsibility, a feeling of lawlessness and escape, accompanied by a little dizziness and perhaps a tendency to giggle out loud. I did not have in mind the ceiling spinning like a great plate somebody had thrown at me, nor the pale green blobs of the chairs swelling, converging, disintegrating, playing with me a game full of enormous senseless inanimate malice. My head sank back; I closed my eyes. And at once opened them, opened them wide, threw myself out of the chair and down the hall and reached—thank God, thank God—the Berrymans' bathroom, where I was sick everywhere, everywhere, and dropped like a stone.

From this point on I have no continuous picture of what happened; my memories of the next hour or two are split into vivid and improbable segments, with nothing but murk and uncertainty between. I do remember lying on the bathroom floor looking sideways at the little six-sided white tiles, which lay together in such an admirable and logical pattern, seeing them with the brief broken gratitude and sanity of one who has just been torn to pieces with vomiting. Then I remember sitting on the stool in front of the hall phone, asking weakly for Joyce's number. Joyce was not home. I was told by her mother (a rather rattlebrained woman, who didn't seem to notice a thing the matter—for which I felt weakly, mechanically grateful) that she was at Kay Stringer's house. I didn't know Kay's number so I just asked the operator; I felt I couldn't risk looking down at the telephone book.

Kay Stringer was not a friend of mine but a new friend of Joyce's. She had a vague reputation for wildness and a long switch of hair, very oddly, though naturally, coloured—from soap-yellow to caramel-brown. She knew a lot of boys more exciting than Martin Collingwood, boys who had quit school or been imported into town to play on the hockey team. She and Joyce rode around in these boys' cars, and sometimes went with them—having lied of course to their mothers—to the Gay-la dance hall on the highway north of town.

I got Joyce on the phone. She was very keyed-up, as she always was with boys around, and she hardly seemed to hear what I was saying.

"Oh, I can't tonight," she said. "Some kids are here. We're going to play cards. You know Bill Kline? He's here. Ross Armour—"

"I'm *sick*," I said, trying to speak distinctly; it came out an inhuman croak. "I'm *drunk*, Joyce!" Then I fell off the stool and the receiver dropped out of my hand and banged for a while dismally against the wall.

I had not told Joyce where I was, so after thinking about it for a moment she phoned my mother, and using the elaborate and unnecessary subterfuge that young girls delight in, she found out. She and Kay and the boys—there were three of them—told some story about where they were going to Kay's mother, and got into the car and drove out. They found me still lying on the broadloom carpet in the hall; I had been sick again, and this time I had not made it to the bathroom.

It turned out that Kay Stringer, who arrived on this scene only by accident, was exactly the person I needed. She loved a crisis, particularly one like this, which had a shady and scandalous aspect and which must be kept secret from the adult world. She became excited, aggressive, efficient; that energy which was termed wildness was simply the overflow of a great female instinct to manage, comfort and control. I could hear her voice coming at me from all directions, telling me not to worry, telling Joyce to find the biggest coffeepot they had and make it full of coffee (*strong* coffee, she said), telling the boys to pick me up and carry me to the sofa. Later, in the fog beyond my reach, she was calling for a scrubbrush.

Then I was lying on the sofa, covered with some kind of crocheted throw they had found in the bedroom. I didn't want to lift my head. The house was full of the smell of coffee. Joyce came in, looking very pale; she said that the Berryman kids had wakened up but she had given them a cookie and told them to go back to bed, it was all right; she hadn't let them out of their room and she didn't believe they'd remember. She said that she and Kay had cleaned up the bathroom and the hall though she was afraid there was still a spot on the rug. The coffee was ready. I didn't understand anything very well. The boys had turned on the radio and they were going through the Berrymans' record collection; they had it out on the floor. I felt there was something odd about this but I could not think what it was.

Kay brought me a huge breakfast mug full of coffee.

"I don't know if I can," I said. "Thanks."

"Sit up," she said briskly, as if dealing with drunks was an everyday business for her so I had no need to feel myself important. (I met, and recognized, that tone of voice years later, in the maternity ward.) "Now drink," she said. I drank, and at the same time realized that I was wearing only my slip. Joyce and Kay had taken off my blouse and skirt. They had brushed off the skirt and washed out the blouse, since it was nylon; it was hanging in the bathroom. I pulled the throw up under my arms and Kay laughed. She got everybody coffee. Joyce brought in the coffeepot and on Kay's instructions she kept filling my cup whenever I drank from it. Somebody said to me with interest, "You must have really wanted to tie one on."

"No," I said rather sulkily, obediently drinking my coffee. "I only had two drinks."

Kay laughed, "Well it certainly gets to you, I'll say that. What time do you expect *they'll* be back?" she said.

"Late, after one I think."

"You should be all right by that time. Have some more coffee."

Kay and one of the boys began dancing to the radio. Kay danced very sexily, but her face had the gently superior and indulgent, rather cold look it had when she was lifting me up to drink the coffee. The boy was whispering to her and she was smiling, shaking her head. Joyce said she was hungry, and she went out to the kitchen to see what there was—potato chips or crackers, or something like that, that you could eat without making too noticeable a dint. Bill Kline came over and sat on the sofa beside me and patted my legs through the crocheted throw. He didn't say anything to me, just patted my legs and looked at me with what seemed to me a very stupid, half-sick, absurd and alarming expression. I felt very uncomfortable; I wondered how it had ever got around that Bill Kline was so good looking, with an expression like that. I moved my legs nervously and he gave me a look of contempt, not ceasing to pat me. Then I scrambled off the sofa, pulling the throw around me, with the idea of going to the bathroom to see if my blouse was dry. I lurched a little when I started to walk, and for some reason—probably to show Bill Kline that he had not panicked me—I immediately exaggerated this, and calling out, "Watch me walk a straight line!" I lurched and stumbled, to the accompaniment of everyone's laughter, towards the hall. I was standing in the archway between the hall and the living room when the knob of the front door turned with a small matter-of-fact click and everything became silent behind me except the radio of course; and the crocheted throw inspired by some delicate malice of its own slithered down around my feet, and there—oh, delicious moment in a well-organized farce—there stood the Berrymans, Mr. and Mrs., with expressions on their faces as appropriate to the occasion as any old-fashioned director of farces could wish. They must have been preparing those expressions, of course; they could not have produced them in the first moment of shock; with the noise we were making, they had no doubt heard us as soon as they got out of the car; for the same reason, we had not heard them. I don't think I ever knew what brought them home so early—a headache, an argument—and I was not really in a position to ask.

Mr. Berryman drove me home. I don't remember how I got into that car, or how I found my clothes and put them on, or what kind of a good night, if any, I said to Mrs. Berryman. I don't remember what happened to my friends, though I imagine they gathered up their coats and fled, covering up the ignominy of their departure with a mechanical roar of defiance. I remember Joyce with a box of crackers in her hand, saying that I had become terribly sick from eating—I think she said *sauerkraut*—for supper, and that I had called them for help. (When I asked her later what they made of this she said, "It wasn't any use. You *reeked*.") I remember also her saying, "Oh, no, Mr. Berryman I beg of you, my mother is a terribly nervous person. I don't know what the shock might do to her. I will go down on my knees to you if you like but *you must not phone my mother*." I have no picture of her down on her knees—and she would have done it in a minute—so it seems this threat was not carried out.

Mr. Berryman said to me, "Well I guess you know your behaviour tonight is a pretty serious thing." He made it sound as if I might be charged with criminal negligence or something worse. "It would be very wrong of me to overlook it," he said. I suppose that besides being angry and disgusted with *me*, he was worried about taking me home in this condition to my strait-laced parents, who could always say I got the liquor in his house. Plenty of Temperance people would think that enough to hold him responsible, and the town was full of Temperance people. Good relations with the town were very important to him from a business point of view.

"I have an idea it wasn't the first time," he said. "If it was the first time, would a girl be smart enough to fill three bottles up with water? No. Well, in this case, she *was* smart enough, but not smart enough to know I could spot it. What do you say to that?" I opened my mouth to answer, and although I was feeling quite sober the only sound that came out was a loud, desolate-sounding giggle. He stopped in front of our house. "Light's on," he said. "Now go in and tell your parents the straight truth. And if you don't, remember I will." He did not mention paying me for my baby-sitting services of the evening and the subject did not occur to me either.

I went into the house and tried to go straight upstairs but my mother called to me. She came into the front hall, where I had not turned on the light, and she must have smelled me at once for she ran forward with a cry of pure amazement, as if she had seen somebody falling, and caught me by the shoulders as I did indeed fall down against the banister, overwhelmed by my fantastic lucklessness, and I told her everything from the start, not omitting even the name of Martin Collingwood and my flirtation with the aspirin bottle, which was a mistake.

On Monday morning my mother took the bus over to Baileyville and found the liquor store and bought a bottle of Scotch whisky. Then she had to wait for a bus back, and she met some people she knew and she was not quite able to hide the bottle in her bag; she was furious with herself for not bringing a proper shopping bag. As soon as she got back she walked out to the Berrymans'; she had not even had lunch. Mr. Berryman had not gone back to the factory. My mother went in and had a talk with both of them and made an excellent impression and then Mr. Berryman drove her home. She talked to them in the forthright and unemotional way she had, which was always agreeably surprising to people prepared to deal with a mother, and she told them that although I seemed to do well enough at school I was extremely backward—or perhaps eccentric—in my emotional development. I imagine that this analysis of my behaviour was especially effective with Mrs. Berryman, a great reader of Child Guidance books. Relations between them warmed to the point where my mother brought up a specific instance of my difficulties, and disarmingly related the whole story of Martin Collingwood.

Within a few days it was all over town and the school that I had tried to commit suicide over Martin Collingwood. But it was already all over school and the town that the Berrymans had come home on Saturday night to find me drunk, staggering, wearing nothing but my slip, in a room with three boys, one of whom was Bill Kline. My mother had said that I was to pay for the bottle she had taken the Berrymans out of my baby-sitting earnings, but my clients melted away like the last April snow, and it would not be paid for yet if newcomers to town had not moved in across the street in July, and needed a baby-sitter before they talked to any of their neighbours.

My mother also said that it had been a great mistake to let me go out with boys and that I would not be going out again until well after my sixteenth birthday, if then. This did not prove to be a concrete hardship at all, because it was at least that long before anybody asked me. If you think that news of the Berrymans' adventure would put me in demand for whatever gambols and orgies were going on in and around that town, you could not be more mistaken. The extraordinary publicity which attended my first debauch may have made me seem marked for a special kind of ill luck, like the girl whose illegitimate baby turns out to be triplets: nobody wants to have anything to do with her. At any rate I had at the same time one of the most silent telephones and positively the most sinful reputation in the whole High School. I had to put up with this until the next fall, when a fat blonde girl in grade ten ran away with a married man and was picked up two months later, living in sin—though not with the same man—in the city of Sault Ste. Marie. Then everybody forgot about me.

But there was a positive, a splendidly unexpected, result of this affair; I got completely over Martin Collingwood. It was not only that he at once said, publicly, that he had always thought I was a nut; where he was concerned I had no pride, and my tender fancy could have found a way around that, a month, a week, before. What was it that brought me back into the world again? It was the terrible and fascinating reality of my disaster; it was *the way things happened.* Not that I enjoyed it; I was a self-conscious girl and I suffered a good deal from all this exposure. But the development of events on that Saturday night—that fascinated me; I felt that I had had a glimpse of the shameless, marvellous, shattering absurdity with which the plots of life, though not of fiction, are improvised. I could not take my eyes off it.

And of course Martin Collingwood wrote his Senior Matric that June and went away to the city to take a course at a school for Morticians, as I think it is called, and when he came back he went into his uncle's undertaking business. We lived in the same town and we would hear most things that happened to each other but I do not think we met face to face or saw one another, except at a distance, for years. I went to a shower for the girl he married, but then everybody went to everybody else's showers. No, I do not think I really saw him again until I came home after I had been married several years, to attend a relative's funeral. Then I saw him; not quite Mr. Darcy but still very nice-looking in those black clothes. And I saw him looking over at me with an expression as close to a reminiscent smile as the occasion would permit, and I knew that he had been surprised by a memory either of my devotion or my little buried catastrophe. I gave him a gentle uncomprehending look in return. I am a grown-up woman now; let him unbury his own catastrophes.

The Sweeper

GAETAN BRULOTTE 1982

Many visitors praise the cleanliness and orderliness of Canadian cities, and Canadians are rightly proud of their reputation as members of a decent and civilized nation. Occasionally, a writer sets out to challenge what society values. In this sardonic tale, a French-speaking author creates a picture of what Canadian city life might just be like if the future should become obsessed with keeping Canada tidy.

We're off. The motorcycle flies away, its chrome dazzling the street, dizzy with speed; it almost soars, as though liberated from gravity's cage, throwing its euphoric challenge to the low and ponderous sky.

The offices have just closed, but the stores are still open. The passersby seem hurried on this late autumn afternoon. The weather is gloomy. The clouds rumble. The wind flaps on its hinges. Leaves flutter their panic and are scattered. The world fills suddenly with meaning.

Red light. Stop. At the line, the idling motorcycle grows impatient. It vibrates and growls jerkily. As if to curse the dense city traffic.

Green. Let's go. Gas pours into the cylinders. Mutterings become a series of explosions. Their noise quickly reaches a peak. The street, lit by its walls of store windows and pulsing to the flash of neon signs, rhythmically inhales a new mass of cars. In and out of this slow-moving herd, the motorcycle dodges—agile, weightless, ethereal. A powerful untamed Pegasus, it prances in the midst of the roadway, refusing to fall into step. With each excess it grows wilder, more triumphant. It ignores both the traffic signs of the city and the indicators on its own dials. The faster it plunges ahead, the more sparks shower out of its flaming exhaust pipe, the more it seems to be becoming flight itself.

Each time he accelerates the pilot breaks more of the bonds holding him to earth, forgets the boring flatness of things and their prison of gravity to taste the joy of ascent. His body is wedded to the machine: a feeling of power lifts him, the noise gives him wings; the ego and the engine fuse to become a single impressive display of pure force. The last earthly limits begin to yield and, hair whipping like a flag, the rider feels that the universe is at his fingertips, his fiefdom. By manipulating a throttle, a clutch and a gearshift, he is suddenly

Shooting a Sitting Bird by John McKinnon, 1981, steel.

akin to the ancient mythological gods who, with a simple gesture, release thunder and wind. From the height of this dominion he weighs also, in his absent-minded way, all the fragility of human creation: his eye, drunk with speed, immediately forgets everything it has succeeded in glimpsing. To him the urban landscape seems a cloth-and-cardboard set put up for one dizzying moment, that of his amnesiac passage. Theatrical façades ready to be taken down fly by on each side and slip into the ephemeral past of the rearview mirror before finally being swallowed by sharp gulps at each new throatful of cool air.

Ah! The exquisite pleasure of speed. To go ever faster, to explore the capacities of a force as elemental as that of an engine. The temptation to accelerate is irresistible, because by constantly living in danger, the pilot gets used to narrowing his margins and with a casual eye measures the gradual shrinking of the gap. Now the motorcycle is running at full speed. It passes a last row of cars to arrive like a whirlwind at a crossing beyond which—finally—there seems to be a path unobstructed.

Suddenly the long peal of a horn pierces the muffled, industrious rumbling of the street. Brakes screech. The grand pandemonium of collision. The crash of broken glass. Everything happens in a quick jumble.

Then everything stops. There is no more movement.

Here and there a few colourless beings are fixed to the spot, as though stitched—so many dolls—in their moleskin bags, and watch—frozen—the spectacle. An accident happens so quickly. It is not easy to understand how these things happen. It's always like that.

There is no movement.

Icarus has lost his wings. Skidding, swerving, the metal horse, in wanting to avoid a pedestrian, leapt sideways, caromed into a car, and rebounded with a flash of chrome into a lamp post. As for the hero of the skies, he has been thrown far away: he lies squashed on the cobblestones, in the gutter, near a sewer, the lower part of his body completely broken. Reality abruptly takes up its cruel solidity and re-establishes its kingdom.

Nevertheless, the bloodied and dishevelled head of the motor-cyclist still stirs. But slowly. Little by little, everything becomes as before. The passersby continue their window shopping and don't even notice what is at their feet. Traffic resumes its rhythm, once more at the crossroads there is that steady alternation of braking and acceleration. The cars manoeuvre more skilfully to avoid the body of the hurt man but, despite all their precautions, some cars inevitably drive over what remains of his legs. As for the ruined motorcycle—it was quickly pushed to the side of the roadway. People do what they can. They really behave very well. Just the same, you can't ask too much of them. This is the time when offices are closing. People want to finish their shopping and get home. That's entirely normal. There's enough work to be done during the day. People have neither the time nor the desire to get involved in somebody else's troubles.

The dying man raises his eyes and—in a final effort—dragging himself through his own blood, tries to pull himself onto the sidewalk because, he has realized, he is blocking traffic. Say what you like, social conscience still survives, even at the heart of the most extreme inner panic.

The vague odour of gasoline released to the street by the fall of the motorcycle doesn't seem to trouble the passersby. That, at least, is some consolation. But suddenly the situation takes a turn for the worse. The sky, overcast all day, gradually opens up and then—as though it had all this time been waiting for the signal—releases a torrential downpour. The drops fall by the thousand, by the million. Mixed with hard white hailstones. The forecast predicted this. Cold rain mixed with hail. The pedestrians, faces pinched, are especially taken by surprise. But the rain makes the merchants happy, because shoppers run for the shelter of the stores. Windshield wipers are turned on. Engines lose patience with the stop light.

The dying man pushes his face into the pavement and tries once again to lever his encumbering body out of the public roadway. But his efforts are in vain. He is unable to move. His hindquarters are stuck to the ground like skin on frozen metal. Exhausted, he still lifts his head and opens his mouth to call or to regain his breath.

Green light. Time to go. The throbbing of the traffic begins again. There is furious honking at that thing in the street. It seems to be a drunk. People curse him, shout at him to get out of the way. His voice wants to reply, but makes no sound.

Because of that stare fixed on me, there is a sudden change in atmosphere: a sudden warmth seems to rise up all around. This broken lump of meat is staring at me, but with a strangely melting plea. I admit that this gaze, in distress, and for that reason forceful, intimidates me—suffering, despite what you hear, is a kind of power. And as it doesn't leave me for an instant, it forces me to act. I lower my eyes and I keep sweeping. I do my work as best can. The boss seldom has reason to reproach me about that. Briefly I yield to weakness once more, and from under my eyelid I look at the dying man. His eyes hover on the edge of consciousness, implore. But what can I do? He is keeping me from my work. What if the boss were to come by? I can already imagine his anger. "Sweep away that mess. That's an order. What are you waiting for? You want me to report you?"

Before, when I was just learning the job, it would have been possible for me to make a mistake. I would have been forgiven on the grounds of inexperience. Before, I could have gone to one side, I could have pretended not to see him. But now it's not possible to ignore him.

"Sweep away that mess! That's an order!" I know my job now. My boss relies on me. So everything must be cleaned. And when you're a professional, as I am, nothing could be simpler. First, take off the manhole cover. Then, holding the broom firmly as if you were scraping up a giant wad of gum, brace the handle under your armpit to make a solid lever—if necessary, pushing with a foot as well—and, shove the thing into the hole. Like that. After that, a few swipes with the broom on the remains with a bit of water. And then it's all gone. Everything is a question of technique. Before, I probably could not have pulled it off. Now, I have attained a certain perfection in my work. That I know, though I might know nothing else. I have my certificate. In a trade, nothing can equal experience: it's something that can't be bought. Ask the boss.

Escalator by Marian Scott, 1936, oil on panel.

Getting Bonded

BRIAN FAWCETT 1984

There are many tales in Canada which celebrate the heroism of ordinary people and the way that they used to wrestle with the harsh climate and wild terrain of Canada in their struggle to survive. But Canada is increasingly a land of cities. What do you have to do, if you want to survive in one of these—especially when you are near the bottom of the pile? The author sardonically wonders whether people might need other types of virtues in this brave new world.

Winter was coming, and I was broke, so I got a job driving truck for one of the soft drink companies. So did Bud, and so did a little guy named Bobby Sondis, which isn't his real name. I can't remember his real name and neither can anyone else. I got the job because I was smart and knew the business, and because I was one of the franchise bottler's sons from upcountry. They thought, I guess, that I was doing it to learn the business, as they say, from the ground up. The truth was that I was confused about what to do with my life. Like most of my generation I didn't know where the ground was or even what it was. I just needed the money, and driving pop trucks was the only work I knew.

Bud got the job because he was an experienced driver-salesman, having worked in the industry on and off since he'd been a teenager. He'd worked for my father for a couple of years, and I liked him. He'd taught me, among other things, most of what I knew about driving trucks, and with less success, how to talk fast when I didn't know what I was doing.

On my first day on the job I was sent right into downtown Vancouver with an eight-pallet flat deck, a Ford cab-forward truck of a type I'd never driven before. I'd never even driven a car in a big city, actually, but I didn't say anything about that to the supervisor who assigned me to the route. He handed me an invoice book and gave me a big burly guy as a swamper. The swamper was several years older than I was, and luckily he knew the route.

I thought I knew the business, but it was a morning for surprises. The first thing I found out was that I was buying my load from the Company every morning, and the Company was going to buy the remains of the load back from me that night when I came in. I was therefore responsible for any thefts, breakage or mistakes in between. The commission was ten cents for every full case I sold, and five cents for every case of empties I brought back, and I was getting a $60 a week basic wage in case my commission didn't turn out to be more than that.

I looked through the route sheets, and it didn't take me long to figure out I would have trouble making more than the basic wage. On a really good summer day, the route sheets said, I might sell 150–200 cases. That meant I would make about $50 a day, which in those days was reasonably good money.

But this was November, and a good day was about sixty cases, which might mean $20–25 a day, and if you dropped a few cases on the street it would come out to considerably less. The swamper told me I'd have to work about the same hours as in the summer, which meant I was getting lousy pay for the hours I'd be working. It also explained why he didn't mind being my swamper—he was making more than I was.

I learned some other things in the first few hours I was on the job. I noticed that the invoices weren't numbered. In my experience they'd always been numbered, and a lost invoice book could put you in deep trouble, because no one knew who you'd sold to, or how much. It prevented you from stealing from the customers, and it made it hard to steal from the Company unless you were in cahoots with one of your customers. Here, the invoices could go anywhere, but because you bought and cashed in your load every day, it was nearly impossible to steal from the Company. So, I figured, given the lousy pay, you were supposed to steal from your customers.

The second thing I learned that day was more disturbing. Halfway through the morning I was intercepted by one of the Company's sales supervisors. He'd come to show me all the things I was doing wrong and to deliver, on the job, the Company Speech. He informed me, after some bullshit about how it was important to please the customers and to work hard, that it was important above all to be honest. I was, he announced proudly, going to Get Bonded.

I had an idea of what that meant. A bonded driver-salesman is one who is certified by an insurance company as fully capable of handling monetary transactions honestly and skillfully. The main reason for doing it is cosmetic. The Company is assuring customers that the Company is a "good" company that hires trustworthy employees. From a driver's point of view it means that if you screw up, you can never be bonded again, and you can't get jobs in a large sector of the service industry.

I had a problem. First, I wasn't going to be making enough to live on. Second, I was going to get bonded at the same time as I was going to have to steal to make a living wage. I mulled it over for a few days and made my decision. There was no point in whining about it. I'd have to steal.

Grafting, as it was called, was easy to learn. The techniques were simple. You took fifteen cases into a supermarket, got the invariably stupid bagboys to check it in, and then you hauled five of them back out and threw them on the truck. Another method was to use empty cases in between and under the full ones. The bagboys never checked to see if the cases you were bringing in were full.

Once you got your graft cases, you sold them to customers who paid cash—usually Chinese grocers. If you grafted ten to fifteen cases a day, you could make a living wage. If you got ambitious, you could make good money. Most of my fellow driver-salesmen, I soon discovered, were very ambitious.

After the first day I was given a route of my own in the east end of the city. It wasn't a good route—most of my customers were small grocers—so I had to steal the few supermarkets on the route blind. After a while there was a certain degree of risk involved. Within a few months, it seemed to me, even an idiot would be able to see what was going on. Officially, at least, I was selling large volumes to the supermarkets, and almost nothing to the small grocers.

Bud got a better route out in the suburbs with better volumes and better opportunities to graft. But he pointed out, when I complained that I felt like a sitting duck, that all the other routes looked the same from the Company's point of view, and that the Company knew what was going on anyway. It was, he said, better than paying people decent wages. Bud just shrugged when I said they were a bunch of assholes for turning us into criminals.

"That's the way things are," he told me. "You're the asshole if you think it's going to be any different."

On his third day at work, Bobby Sondis went around a corner too fast, and half his load went off the side of the truck. By the time he got the mess cleaned up, it had cost him $50. The Company let that one go, but his first paycheque was $36. He dropped his load again before he figured out how to make his truck go around a corner, and he went home the second week with $23. By the sixth week he'd gotten overconfident and did it again—this time right in front of the plant. I drove in ten minutes later, but I didn't stop to help. It was

7 p.m. and it was raining. So far, I knew, Bobby was averaging $40 a week.

Bud and I assumed he was grafting like everyone else. But one night he caught the downtown bus with us after work, and the first thing he asked us was how we made it on the lousy pay.

"It's not so hard," Bud smirked. "How much are you clearing?"

"I dunno. About forty bucks a week," he said.

"How much graft are you taking?" I asked.

Bobby seemed puzzled. "Graft? What are you talking about?"

"Graft," Bud said. "You know. Steal from the rich to get from the poor."

"You have to steal on this job," I said, "or it just isn't worth working."

"How do you manage to steal?" he asked. "The bastards check your load coming and going."

Bud rolled his eyes. "You don't steal from the Company," he said. "You hit the supermarkets and the other big customers, and then you sell what you get to your cash customers. Every driver in the place is doing it."

"That's dishonest," Bobby objected, his small eyes narrowing. Bud and I started laughing. "What if you get caught?"

"Nobody gets caught unless they're totally stupid," I told him. "The Company knows we're doing it. That's why the wages are so low. It's no skin off their asses if we rip one guy off and sell it to somebody else. They still get their money."

The bewilderment in Bobby's face began to lighten into something like hope.

"Will you show me how to do it?" he asked, more of Bud than of me.

Bud nodded. The bus pulled up in front of the Biltmore Hotel and the three of us got off. It was 9 p.m. and we had cash in our pockets—at least Bud and I did. We were going to even things up by showing a working buddy how to score a decent wage, and it felt good.

"C'mon," I said. "I'll buy you a beer."

We got drunk, and Bud and I taught Bobby how to graft. He was a little slow to catch on, but even so, it didn't take very long. Later in the evening Bud told us some stories about the door-to-door bleach business he used to run. Then he told us he had 300 cases of Mission Orange stored in a friend's basement. That company had recently gone out of business, partly because their products tasted lousy, but partly because their drivers had been stealing them blind. A week or so before they folded, Bud had driven his truck over to his friend's place, and unloaded the entire truck. No one knew the difference, he said. I wondered if he'd been doing that to my father, but I didn't think about it too hard or for too long. Bobby's eyes were like saucers.

It wasn't that Bobby was stupid, and it wasn't what most people would call innocence. Bobby thought that when you worked hard you'd get paid a fair wage for it. Bud and I believed that maybe that was how things ought to be, but since we were confronted by an obvious exception to that rule, we didn't hesitate to act on the opportunity that exception provided. Whatever we believed about wage labour and "the system" was superseded by a much stronger conviction that the worst thing that could happen to a man was to be taken for a sucker. We also believed that if an opportunity presented itself, you were supposed to go for it, and the degree of restraint you exercised was pretty flexible. All that stuff about fairness and honesty was fine, but it was like thin ice. If the ice started cracking, you had to know what to do.

I had some private ideas about never ripping off friends, but I never did know where Bud stood on those kinds of questions. Not knowing didn't bother me, but I never really turned my back on him. Bud never turned his back on anyone or anything, and he was proud of it.

Bobby, on the other hand, believed everything he'd learned as a kid about what's good or true. This, I guessed, was his first experience with the way the real world operated, and he wasn't enjoying it. He didn't enjoy what happened next, either.

Two days later, he grafted six cases from a supermarket on the second stop he made, and sold four of them to his next customer, a Chinese grocer a few blocks away. A Company supervisor nailed him for it as he got back into the truck with the $12 cash in his pocket. He was fired on the spot, and told there was a good chance he would be charged. I heard about it when I got back to the plant that night. I'd grafted nine cases myself that day.

The supervisor who'd caught him was sitting around the office, no doubt at the management's instruction, bragging about it. His main point seemed to be that Bobby was a lousy driver and a wimp, and that he therefore deserved to be canned. The Company, he said unctuously, had suspicions that he was grafting, and had been watching him.

"That sawed-off sonofabitch will never get bonded again," he smirked. He'd told Bud privately that the Company had decided that the grafting was getting out of hand, and that they wanted to make an example of someone. He'd hinted that they'd hired Bobby more or less for that purpose.

"No use screwing up someone who could turn into a good driver-salesman," he'd said.

"What a bunch of dirty bastards," I said to Bud when he related the story to me.

Bud shrugged it off. "No use getting upset about it," he said. "But it's kind of a piss-off that we were the guys who told him how to do it."

The Christmas season was coming, and that meant a big push in the industry to get the customers to load up on mixers. A special system was set up so that customers could stock up without paying for it until after the Christmas season was over. The Company held a sales meeting for the drivers, setting up quotas for each route. The quotas were ridiculously high, with small cash prizes for the first three drivers to reach 50, 75, and 100% of their quotas.

It was with these quotas that the Company made their first and maybe their only mistake. The quotas provided a unique opportunity for us to screw the Company. Theoretically, you could load your customers up as much as you wanted, and you could make good commissions doing it. But if you oversold, you had to haul it back out again in January, and there was a reverse commission.

There were two loopholes in the set-up. The first one was obvious. It naturally afforded unusual opportunities for graft. It was common custom that during the first two weeks of the customer-loading period there were no cash sales turned in to the Company. It was, I heard, tacitly acknowledged as a Christmas bonus. But Bud spotted another more lucrative and totally legal way of cashing in.

I was bitter about the way Bobby Sondis had been treated, and I didn't hide it very well, least of all from Bud. I threatened to quit, and it must have been one of my tirades about quitting that tipped him off. On the bus going to work one morning early into the season he asked me if I was interested in screwing the Company, but good.

"Sure I am," I said.

"Well," he said, "then don't quit, and stop yapping about it."

I asked him why, and he grinned. "We're going to screw the Company on the level, and they won't be able to do a goddam thing about it."

"Oh, sure," I said, sceptically, "I'd love that. How?"

"We're going to load our customers up until they've got mixers under their beds, and then we're going to quit and let the Company haul it all back. We get our commissions, and they won't be able to touch us. They'll have to pay someone overtime to do the hauling. We'll be screwing them double."

Four days later Bud hit 50% of his quota. He did it without turning in a single cash sale, and only one other driver had reached 25% of theirs. The other driver was me, and I was close to 40% of mine. Bud had 75% before anyone but me reached 40%, and he reached 100% by the time the rest got to half. Three days before Christmas he was close to doubling his quota. I'd reached mine and was closing in on Bud. No other driver was close to us.

That night the Company threw a party in the back of the plant, and treated us all to cheap rye in paper cups. Bud and I collected our bonus money and our commission cheques, and drank their cheap rye. The supervisors were ecstatic over our performance, even though one of the other drivers was upset because Bud had been servicing customers on his route. Bud was leaving for San Francisco the next day, but I was the only one who knew. I had a bus ticket to go home in my pocket, and even Bud didn't know that. We grinned a lot, drank our rye and said nothing. We were ready to leave when the regional manager showed up.

He was one of those people who talk in capital letters. "Everybody Hold On for a Few Minutes here," he yelled. "We have Some Door Prizes here for our Top Achievers."

I was about to walk out, but Bud stopped me. As far as he was concerned it was another opportunity, and he wasn't about to let us pass it up.

"Can We have our Big Three over here, Puleeaase."

Bud, the other winning driver and I shuffled over to where Capital Letters had set himself up. He was actually standing on a pop case. He was a short man, but he didn't remind me much of Bobby Sondis. I wondered what Bobby was doing at that moment.

"If you Gentlemen will Step around the Corner, you'll Find your Door Prizes Waiting for you," he said, moving his arms and body as if he was the M.C. on a T.V. game show.

Behind several pallets of empty bottles were three doors, each with a wire rack attached to it. The racks held a roll of toilet paper. Each door had a name on it, and we dutifully went over and picked up our doors and walked back out to the jeers and laughter of the losers. Capital Letters was grinning broadly, and he shook hands with each of us.

"Seriously, Men, I want you to know that the Company is Proud of You," he said to everyone and to no one, "Merry Christmas and Use these Well. They might be the Doors to Success."

I was going to tell him what he could do with his door prize and his job and his phoney glad-handing good cheer, but Bud grabbed my arm.

"Let it go," he said quietly. "He's a jerk, and we're getting out of here. It ain't going to change. Let's just take what they gave us and go."

A few minutes later we were walking to the bus stop outside the plant, waiting for the last bus we would catch to or from anywhere near that place. We'd each left a note in the supervisor's mailbox with our name and simple message: "I quit".

I never got bonded again so I don't know if the Company tried to do anything about the way we screwed them. Probably they did nothing. I don't know what became of Bud because I never saw him again. I don't know what happened to Bobby Sondis either. The Company closed the plant some years ago because the employees unionized. I remember thinking the next day on the bus back north that it didn't feel very much like Christmas, and that the small bond of trust I had with the way things were was broken forever.

The Knife Sharpener

BONNIE BURNARD 1988

Canada has become one of the most prosperous nations in the world, with an especially high standard of living among the many people who live in the sprawling, prosperous and seemingly tranquil suburbs of its major cities—but what would happen if one family's pleasant, secure way of living was suddenly, dangerously threatened?

"Now tell me again," Janet said, wrapping the yellow scarf around her daughter's neck. Erin was dark, like her mother, with unruly curly hair framing an open face. She began her singsong.

"Don't dawdle, don't play with the dogs, don't talk to anyone I don't know. Go right to Kathleen's house." Kathleen was the twelve-year-old daughter of a friend and she had agreed to walk Erin to school the first year.

"Right," Janet opened the back door. "Off you go. See you at lunch." Mitsy ran up with Daniel in tow.

"Kiss and hug," she demanded. "Kiss and hug for me."

Daniel threw himself into the huddle, his arms raised and eager. After a minute Janet broke them up. "Okay, okay, enough." She herded the little ones back into the den. "Play," she said.

Erin stood hanging on the doorknob, waiting for her mother's hug. She accepted it like a talisman, safer after. "Love you Mom. Bye." She hurried down the steps.

Janet closed the door. She walked back up through the kitchen, grabbed her cigarettes and went to the living room window. From there she could watch Erin march down the driveway and across the street, making her way to the corner, where she turned out of sight. The neighbour, the older woman whose children were grown, sometimes watched Erin too. She'd told Janet that the child walked just like her mother. It was a kind of hurried saunter, a shuffle, anything but graceful. Janet lit her cigarette. Here and there, patches of the road had been worn by traffic to blue-black ice. The smaller kids on the street ran to those patches, sliding as fast and as far as they could, but always later in the morning, when the neighbourhood traffic had ceased and the street was quiet. For the past few years Janet and the other mothers had taken

Kitchen Door with Esther by Christiane Pflug, 1965, oil on canvas.

informal turns supervising the play and even when she was not on patrol, pacing and jumping in her parka and mukluks, she watched from the living room window. This year Erin would not be involved in the games. She was off, on her own.

Mitsy and Daniel stood with Janet now, their hands pressed against the cold window. Mitsy wrapped her arms around her mother's leg. "Time for toast," she said.

Daniel joined in, happy to hear a word he could echo. "Toast," he said. "Toast, toast, toast and jam."

"Okay." Janet took a hand in each of her own. "Let's do it."

The kids hauled themselves up to their places at the table while Janet dropped some bread into the toaster and eased the handle down to catch. She got the peanut butter and jam out and cleared Erin's cereal and juice away. The kids sat quietly, eyeing each other. Any minute some squabble would break out and then in another minute they would be best friends again. It would go on like that all day. She wondered when real long-lasting malice would begin. She'd seen hints of it in Erin, big hints.

The toast popped up.

"There it is," Daniel yelled.

She made herself a cup of coffee and sat down with them. Erin will be in school by now, she thought, will be taking off her coat and scarf and boots and sitting down at her desk, ready.

When the kids had finished eating she took them to the TV in the den. They settled down in front of "Romper Room," waiting for their instructions from the young woman who would lead them through their romps. Janet looked at the woman's perfect face. "You do a fine job," she said. "You're a good broad."

She spoke to the backs on the floor. "I'm going up to shower now. I'll leave the bathroom door open." They ignored her.

She hurried upstairs and made the beds. One of her husband's jackets hung on the bedroom door. That meant it needed a button; the button would be in the pocket. She stripped in the hall, tossing her nightie down the chute before going to the bathroom to turn on the water. Then back to the top of the stairs to listen for any noise other than the voice of Miss whatever-her-name-was on TV. Then into the shower. She sudsed her hair and groaned into the steamy water. Someday she would stand there for an hour, just stand, steaming, wasting water.

Afterwards, downstairs to check the kids and downstairs again to the wash in the basement. Left, right, white, coloured; left, right, white, coloured. She threw the white into the washer. Then upstairs to the bananas. They were past eating raw, ready to be made into muffins. She'd do this, check the mail, have another coffee. Then the kids. Hold them. Tell them there would be muffins.

She was mashing the bananas when the back doorbell rang. Oh go away, she thought, leave me be. But she went to the door and opened it. It was an old man.

"Yes?" she said.

"Morning." He tipped an imaginary hat to her. "I was wondering if you'd have any knives that could use sharpening?"

He was tall but his shoulders were stooped under the sloppy sleeves of a heavy grey curling sweater. It was not zippered and she could see suspenders. They held up dingy brown draped pants, the kind the young guys were wearing again now, but these were from some former life in the world of fashion. A satchel hung over his shoulder, bulky with something heavy. His face, fleshier than the rest of him, was a sickly, ashen colour. Her eyes finally settled on his. They were clear and alert, under bushy grey eyebrows. Well, he's not a drunk, she thought.

"Knives?" she asked.

"Maybe you've heard from your neighbours. I come round every March. Do mowers as well." He bundled his sweater around his chest, moving his weight from one foot to the other.

"Come in," Janet said. "You're cold." She closed the door behind him. "I guess I likely have some that aren't as sharp as they might be. How much do you charge?"

"That's up to you, Mrs.," he said.

Janet started toward the kitchen. "Come this way. I'll give you the knives. The mower's in the basement."

Mitsy and Daniel erupted from their play trance. "Hi," Mitsy said, "Who are you?"

Janet shooed them away from the knife sharpener. She led him to the kitchen drawer and handed him the knives, one after another. "These, I guess."

Downstairs in the basement, she pointed to her husband's workshop. "The mower's in there. I'll leave you to it."

She watched him look around. He dragged a lawn chair over to the workbench, opened his satchel and took out his whetstone.

Janet went to the washer, emptied the white load into the dryer, threw in the coloured and left him to go upstairs. The kids were busy with Lego. She finished the muffins.

Then Mitsy was at her knees.

"Hi, sweetheart," she said. "I'm coming to sit with you." She led her by the hand down into the den. They sat on the floor with Daniel and he pointed to the abstraction he'd built. "Tree," he said.

She played with them, letting them roll over and around her like bear cubs. Between squeals, she could hear from the basement the rhythmic scrape of steel against whetstone. She wondered if he could hear the squeals. The timer buzzed.

"Muffins!" she said.

The kids ran ahead of her, stopping just short of the stove. She pushed them back so she could open the oven door. "They have to cool a bit." She dumped the pans upside-down on the counter. Steam rushed up to her face and a sweet banana smell filled the kitchen. The kids danced around her. "In a minute," she said.

She put the kettle on for tea. He can likely smell the muffins, she thought. She reached for the cups and got the tray out from behind the spices. Two hands reached up over the counter and she put a steaming muffin in each. "Blow on them," she warned. "I'm going downstairs. You eat your muffins with Big Bird." They wandered off, watching their muffins as they carried them.

When the tea was ready, she arranged the pot and cups on the tray with a plate of muffins and carried it down to him. He was bent over his work, his knees braced under his thickly muscled arms. He didn't see her until she was right in front of him. He jumped a little.

"Thought you might like some tea and muffins." She put the tray on the workbench.

"Don't mind if I do," he said. He set the knife he was working on down beside him on the floor, the whetstone on his lap. "This is one fine old house," he said. "Tell by the shape of the basement." He waited for her to pour his tea.

"Yes," she said. "It's got some creaks and cracks but we like it." She leaned against the wall.

He took a muffin. "What line of work's your husband in?" he asked.

"He's an architect," she answered.

"That'd be interesting," he nodded.

"Are you retired from something?" Janet asked. "I'm guessing this is sort of a hobby?"

He leaned back to give her room as she poured his tea. "Retired from a lot of things," he chuckled. "Never been very lucky with a career." He took a sip of tea and added some milk. "Had jobs, though. Some good, some not so good."

Janet thought about her father. He'd been lucky; he'd made it. All the men in her life had made it, one way or another.

"I quit regular work when my wife died," he said. "She needed money more than I ever did."

"I'm sorry," Janet offered.

"Oh, that's all right," he said. "We didn't get along anyway. She spent most of her time hanging over a Bingo card, anxious for the big win. Did make a good pot of tea, though. Like you. I miss a woman pouring my tea."

"You have children?" Janet asked.

"Two," he said. "The young lady took off with the scum of the earth when she was sixteen and my boy's over in the North Sea, drilling for oil. He don't write much but I follow the papers to see what's going on over there. His mother used to worry over him but I don't. He's a hell of a swimmer. If the thing threatened to blow, he'd be the first one off, guaranteed." He broke a muffin open and wiped his mouth with the sleeve of his sweater.

Janet saw that the cuff was unravelling, eating away at itself. "That would be a good high-paying job for a young man," she said.

"He's not so young," he said. "He came home two years ago to bury his mother and he was thirty-five then."

Janet was sorry she'd poured a cup for herself and she finished it quickly.

He put his teacup on the tray. "Thanks a million," he said. He picked up his whetstone. "I better get to work here."

"And I better get back upstairs," Janet said. "My oldest will be home soon. I'll leave the muffins for you."

"How old's she?" the knife sharpener asked.

"Six," Janet answered.

"That's a nice age," he said.

She left him to finish, got the clothes out of the dryer and put the coloured load in. Upstairs, she dumped the clothes on the floor with the kids and began to fold. The back door flew open.

Erin ran across the rug and threw herself into the mess of clothes and arms on the floor. "I'm home," she said.

"Boots off," Janet said. "How was school this morning?"

Erin trudged back to the door, kicking off her boots. "We did art," she said. "Real art."

The kids looked at something behind Janet. It was the knife sharpener.

"Finished," he said.

"Oh, good," Janet got up from the floor. "I'll get my purse."

Erin came back into the room. "You're not the plumber," she said.

"No," he answered. "I just had tea with your mommy and sharpened some things for her."

Janet stood beside him, offering a ten dollar bill. "Is this all right?"

"That's good, Mrs. Thank you."

Erin had come to stand in front of her mother, wrapping Janet's arms around her chest.

"I was wondering if you'd like to stay and have lunch with us?" Janet asked. "Just soup."

"No," he said. "I'll be off, thank you." He walked over to the door, turning to wave at the kids as he let himself out.

They all admired Erin's school work, her bold triangles and shaky circles, then Janet went up to put the soup on to heat. She saw the knives on the counter. She was glad she'd had them sharpened. They were overdue. She gathered them up in a bunch and put them into an upper cupboard. They'd have to stay there for a while; the kids wouldn't know how sharp they were until one of them was cut and bleeding.

After lunch, Janet stood at the living room window again, watching Erin, admiring the way she swung her book bag. As the child crossed the street, she took a good run at a sheet of ice, skidding across it and tripping up onto the sidewalk. Erin, the name book said: a fair jewel set in a tranquil sea. Janet wondered if hard work and luck would bring her a good old age with her children. She wondered about the places downtown that offered some warmth, some company. Old hotels, there were six or seven of them, close to the Bay.

She saw him clearly, standing at the corner, his hand outstretched to Erin. Erin gave a little skip then took his hand; Janet had seen her take her grandfather's hand just that way. They walked together around the corner.

She ran back to Mitsy and Daniel in the den. They were watching "Mister Rogers". "Don't move," she said. "I just have to go out for a minute."

She grabbed her coat from the closet and was out the door and half-way down the driveway before she had it on. She ran as hard as she could, down to the corner and around it. Nothing. They were gone. There were two lanes mid-way down the block, one going south, one north, back toward the house. Don't call her name, she told herself. Don't call her name. There are garages, empty yards, shrubs to hide in. She decided on the lane going south. That's where he'd take her. She ran across the street. Her slippers were slapping hard on the icy pavement, loud. She kicked them off and started down the lane in her stockinged feet. She looked in the yards on each side as she ran, looked in every filthy garage window, in every overgrown space between house and fence.

She saw Erin's scarf snagged around the stuccoed corner of a garage twenty yards ahead. She let loose, let everything she had go to her legs.

She found Erin tucked into an evergreen hedge. The knife sharpener was crouched down talking to her in a gentle old man's voice. Janet pulled her away from him, turning the small face into the front of her coat.

The knife sharpener stood up and started to back away from them. "I wouldn't have hurt her, Mrs."

"Just what the hell would you have done with her then? Just what the hell do you think . . ." Janet heard the ugly edge to her voice and she knew she'd have to stop. Erin had taken her hand.

The knife sharpener was edging back, along the wall of the garage. "Please don't call the police," he said.

"What choice do I have?" Janet asked. She saw Erin watching, listening.

They turned their backs on him, walking down the lane and out into the street. She found her slippers there, overturned in the snow and she put them on. Erin hadn't said anything. Just keep quiet, Janet told herself, let her questions sort themselves out. She'll ask the right one. They were nearly at Kathleen's house.

"I shouldn't have gone with him, should I?" Erin looked down at her boots. "He was a stranger."

"No," Janet said. "You shouldn't have. You can know strangers a little bit but they're still strangers."

Erin kicked at the snow. "I thought he was a friend of yours."

Kathleen ran noisily towards them. "Where've you been?" she asked. "My mom's been phoning. We're late. C'mon."

"Hi," Erin said calmly, as though nothing had happened to her. She took her friend's hand. "See you later, Mom."

"Wait, Kathleen," Janet put her hand on the girl's book bag. "You be sure you don't talk to anyone you don't know. All right?"

"I never do. What's wrong?" she asked.

"Just make sure, that's all. I'll talk to your mom this afternoon." Janet watched the two of them go off down the street. Erin was leaning, just slightly, into Kathleen's shoulder. She turned back toward the house and, remembering Mitsy and Daniel, began to run again.

They were fine. They had all the muffins, some half eaten, spread out around them on the floor. "Mister Rogers" was still on. Janet looked at the screen, at his kind face, at his kind cardigan sweater. She felt her feet stinging from the cold.

She went to the living room window with her cigarettes. The snow on the lawns was blue-white in the sun and the black ice on the street had been covered with a light dusting of snow she hadn't seen fall.

She had choices. She could call her husband, who would likely call the police. She could describe the knife sharpener. She could make it so bad for him that he'd never show his face in their world again. Or she could say absolutely nothing, to anyone, ever.

She could take a calm liberal stance. She could get in the Toyota and find him, talk to him, listen to him. She could remind him of his own daughter, when she was small and trusting on his knee. Before she took off with the scum of the earth.

Or she could take the grey ceramic ashtray from the coffee table and hurl it across the room at the fireplace where it would shatter and come to rest in pieces among the ashes.

Cultural Mosaic

Nipikti the Old Man Carver

ALOOTOOK IPELLIE 1976

There was a time when Inuit artists carved small sculptures for themselves. Some were made as toys for their children. Some were made in order to celebrate the people's deep belief in a world in which everything, even a stone, was inhabited by a soul and a personality. Nowadays, their spiritual art has also become a craft, a means of staying alive as they sell their stone carvings at the local co-operative, for strangers in the big cities to buy. How does an old Inuit, long past his hunting days, deal with having to sell his art in an increasingly Westernized world?

Nipikti was now an old man and took three times as long as any young Inuk to get from one point to another. Almost every week, he would get up from his small carving studio at home and start walking out to the Co-op where he sold at least a half a dozen carvings he had finished during the week. He hung the bag of carvings over his shoulder and started out the door, his walking stick leading the way for him.

"This is the day I will get the upper hand of the deal with the Co-op manager. I have no doubt that he will fall in love with the carving I finished today," he said as he closed the door behind himself.

On the way to the Co-op, Nipikti would stop several times to rest his tired old legs by sitting on the same rocks he had sat on for the last twenty years or so.

"Ahhh! Hi, Ojagajaak, it feels good to rest on you," he would say to the first rock, as if the rock was an old friend of his. "These legs of mine are a little weaker than last week, so I will have to sit on you for an extra five minutes if you do not mind."

There he sat to rest on Ojagajaak and looked across the land where he had lived as a young man. That is the place where he had hunted the good animals of the land. That is where he had taken care of his wife and family when they were growing up. "Those were good times of the past," he thought, "times when carvings like these were toys and tokens to us Inuit."

He got up slowly and continued on to the Co-op where he would get the money to support his family. The Co-op was still quite far away.

Dream Figure by Enoya, a Neteselk Eskimo, sculpturing four different animal figures integrated in one shape.

"If I had my way, I would prefer to carve the stones and ivory to make toys for my children, and hunt the animals like I used to. I wasn't such a bad hunter in those days," Nipikti said to himself.

"I never thought I would be living off the very carvings I used to make only to keep my children happy."

Nipikti finally came to the rock where he sat to rest the second time along the way to the Co-op and said, "How are you today Ojagakaluk? I have come again to rest on you. I am an old man now, you know."

He sat on Ojagakaluk and took enough rest there to make it to the next rock. "I shall see you again on my way back. Just make sure the bulldozer doesn't push you under before then," Nipikti shouted back to the second rock as he slowly started walking on.

When he came to the third rock, he sat down and said, "You know, Ojagakutaaq, you are probably the most comfortable rock I have ever sat on in my life. I must say I will certainly miss you the day they remove you from this spot to make way for the new road. You have been a good rock to me and I must thank you in case they start building the road while I am at the Co-op."

He then got up to walk the last leg of the trip to the local Co-op and said to himself that it was time to think about how much he would persuade the Co-op manager to pay him for his carvings. Especially for the good one he finished earlier that day.

"I should be able to sell the good carving for $150 easily," he said. "I'm sure there isn't any other carving this week that was done any better than this one."

When he got to the Co-op, Nipikti took the six carvings out of the bag and laid them on the desk for the manager to look at.

The manager picked up the carvings one by one and looked them over carefully. When he came to the carving Nipikti had done that day, he immediately offered Nipikti $120 for it.

Nipikti stood leaning on his walking stick and counted on $150 as planned. Nipikti knew by experience that the carving was worth that much or even more. "$150," he said.

The manager looked up at Nipikti's face, then picked up the carving in question and mused over the fine detail of the work Nipikti had done. "Okay," he finally said, "I'll give you $130 for it."

Nipikti looked at the manager's face and thought about the last offer for $130. "If you think you are going to play games with me, you might as well be prepared to do it for the rest of the day. I am not going to play that long," he said in Inuktitut.

The manager clearly understood that Nipikti was not about to change his original asking price of $150. He knew that the price was right for the carving. But he decided to try once more to buy the carving for less than that. "140," he said.

Nipikti just stood there and cleared his throat, then said for the last time, "150." And with that, he tapped the top of the desk with his right hand. It was a sign that he meant business.

At that moment, the manager decided to give up trying to persuade the old carver to say yes to what he wanted and agreed to pay the $150 he was asking for.

Nipikti had won the battle this time around. He took the money for the carvings he'd brought in and went out the door to begin his journey back home with his walking stick in hand and money in his pocket to support the family for the next few weeks. He looked across the land and saw that the three rocks where he sat to rest each week were still there. No one had started to build the road yet. And he just smiled and said to himself that it was good.

"I had better make sure that they do not bulldoze my rocks away. The way I see it, I am sure to win my case over that too," he said for the last time, and he slowly moved on toward home where he would start the next carving.

Nipikti the old man carver lives on.

Flowers for Weddings and Funerals

SANDRA BIRDSELL 1982

Although many immigrants to Canada settled there long ago, they and their descendants have retained their original homeland's way of life and its old values. Tolerating and encouraging this sense of belonging has been one of Canada's great strengths. But life is not always so simple, especially if you are young and are aware that Canada is also a changing and even restless society. In this tale, a girl finds herself torn between her loyalty to the old ways of her Russian grandmother and the more exciting life which some people of her own age seem to offer.

My Omah supplies flowers for weddings and funerals. In winter, the flowers come from the greenhouse she keeps warm with a woodstove as long as she can; and then the potted begonias and asters are moved to the house and line the shelves in front of the large triple-pane window she had installed when Opah died so that she could carry on the tradition of flowers for weddings and for funerals. She has no telephone. Telephones are the devil's temptation to gossip and her God admonishes widows to beware of that exact thing.

And so I am the messenger. I bring requests to her, riding my bicycle along the dirt road to her cottage that stands watermarked beneath its whitewash because it so foolishly nestles too close to the Red River.

A dozen or two glads please, the note says. The bride has chosen coral for the colour of her wedding and Omah adds a few white ones because she says that white is important at a wedding. She does not charge for this service. It is unthinkable to her to ask for money to do this thing which she loves.

She has studied carefully the long rows of blossoms to find perfect ones with just the correct number of buds near the top, and laid them gently on newspaper. She straightens and absently brushes perspiration from her brow. She frowns at the plum tree in the corner of the garden where the flies hover in the heat waves. Their buzzing sounds and the thick humid air make me feel lazy. But she never seems to notice the heat, and works tirelessly.

"In Russia," she says as she once more bends to her task, "we made jam. Wild plum jam to put into fruit pockets and platz." Her hands, brown and earth-stained, feel for the proper place to cut into the last gladiolus stalk.

She gathers the stalks into the crook of her arm, coral and white gladioli,

Daughter of Canadian Ukrainian Pioneer by Molly Lenhardt, 1978, oil on canvas-board.

large icy-looking petals that are beaded with tears. Babies' tears, she told me long ago. Each convex drop holds a perfectly shaped baby. The children of the world who cry out to be born are the dew of the earth.

For a long time afterward, I imagined I could hear the garden crying and when I told her this, she said it was true. All of creation cries and groans, you just cannot hear it. But God does.

Poor God. I squint at the sun because she has also said He is Light and I have grown accustomed to the thought that the sun is His eye. To have to face that every day. To have to look down and see a perpetually twisting, writhing, crying creation. The trees have arms uplifted, beseeching. Today I am not sure I can believe it, the way everything hangs limp and silent in the heat.

I follow her back to the house, thinking that perhaps tonight, after the wedding, there will be one less dewdrop in the morning.

"What now is a plum tree but a blessing to the red ants and flies only?" She mutters to herself and shakes dust from her feet before she enters the house. When she speaks her own language, her voice rises and falls like a butterfly on the wind as she smooths over the guttural sounds. Unlike my mother, who does not grow gladioli or speak the language of her youth freely, but with square, harsh sounds, Omah makes a sonatina.

While I wait for her to come from the house, I search the ground beneath the tree to try to find out what offends her so greatly. I can see red ants crawling over sticky, pink pulp, studying the dynamics of moving one rotting plum.

"In Russia, we ate gophers and some people ate babies." I recall her words as I pedal back towards the town. The glads are in a pail of water inside my wire basket. Cool spikelets of flowers seemingly spread across my chest. Here I come. Here comes the bride, big, fat and wide. Where is the groom? Home washing diapers because the baby came too soon.

Laurence's version of that song reminds me that he is waiting for me at the river.

"Jesus Christ, wild plums, that's just what I need," Laurence says and begins pacing up and down across the baked river bank. His feet lift clay tiles as he paces and I squat waiting, feeling the nylon filament between my fingers, waiting for something other than the river's current to tug there at the end of it.

I am intrigued by the patterns the sun has baked into the river bank.

Octagonal shapes spread down to the willows. How this happens, I don't know. But it reminds me of a picture I have seen in Omah's Bible or geography book, something old and ancient like the tile floor in a pharaoh's garden. It is re-created here by the sun on the banks of the Red River.

"What do you need plums for?"

"Can't you see," he says. "Wild plums are perfect to make wine."

I wonder at the tone of his voice when it is just the two of us fishing. He has told me two bobbers today instead of one and the depth of the stick must be screwed down into the muck just so. Only he can do it. And I never question as I would want to because I am grateful to him for the world he has opened up to me. If anyone should come and join us here, Laurence would silently gather his line in, wind it around the stick with precise movements that are meant to show his annoyance, but really are a cover for his sense of not belonging. He would move further down the bank or walk up the hill to the road and his bike. He would turn his back on me, the only friend he has.

I have loved you since grade three, my eyes keep telling him. You, with your lice crawling about your thickly matted hair. My father, being the town's barber, would know, Laurence. But I defied him and played with you anyway.

It is of no consequence to Laurence that daily our friendship drives wedges into my life. He stops pacing and stands in front of me, hands raised up like a preacher's hands.

"Wild plums make damned good wine. My old man has a recipe."

I turn over a clay tile and watch an earthworm scramble to bury itself, so that my smile will not show and twist down inside him.

Laurence's father works up north cutting timber. He would know about wild plum wine. Laurence's mother cooks at the hotel because his father seldom sends money home. Laurence's brother is in the navy and has a tattoo on his arm. I envy Laurence for the way he can take his time rolling cigarettes, never having to worry about someone who might sneak up and look over his shoulder. I find it hard to understand his kind of freedom. He will have the space and time to make his wine at leisure.

"Come with me." I give him my hand.

Omah bends over in the garden. Her only concession to the summer's heat has been to roll her nylon stockings to her ankles. They circle her legs in neat coils. Her instep is swollen, mottled blue with broken blood vessels. She gathers tomatoes in her apron.

Laurence hesitates. He stands away from us with his arms folded across his chest as though he were bracing himself against extreme cold.

"His mother could use the plums," I tell Omah. Her eyes brighten and her tanned wrinkles spread outwards from her smile. She half-runs like a goose to her house with her apron bulging red fruit.

"See," I say to Laurence, "I told you she wouldn't mind."

When Omah returns with pails for picking, Laurence's arms hang down by his sides.

"You tell your Mama," she says to Laurence, "that it takes one cup of sugar to one cup of juice for the jelly." Her English is broken and she looks like any peasant standing in her bedroom slippers. She has hidden her beautiful white hair beneath a kerchief.

She's not what you think, I want to tell Laurence and erase that slight bit of derision from his mouth. Did you know that in their village they were once very wealthy? My grandfather was a teacher. Not just a teacher, but he could have been a professor here at a university.

But our heads are different. Laurence would not be impressed. He has never asked me about myself. We are friends on his territory only.

I beg Laurence silently not to swear in front of her. Her freckled hands pluck fruit joyfully.

"In the old country, we didn't waste fruit. Not like here where people let it fall to the ground and then go to the store and buy what they could have made for themselves. And much better too."

Laurence has sniffed out my uneasiness. "I like home-made jelly," he says. "My mother makes good crabapple jelly."

She studies him with renewed interest. When we each have a pail full of the dust-covered fruit, she tops it with a cabbage and several of the largest unblemished tomatoes I have ever seen.

"Give my regards to your Mama," she says, as though some bond has been established because this woman makes her own jelly.

We leave her standing at the edge of the road shielding her eyes against the setting sun. She waves and I am so proud that I want to tell Laurence about the apple that is named for her. She had experimented with crabapple trees for years and in recognition of her work, the experimental farm has given a new apple tree her name.

"What does she mean, give her regards?" Laurence asks and my intentions are lost in the explanation.

When we are well down the road and the pails begin to get heavy, we stop to rest. I sit beside the road and chew the tender end of a foxtail.

Laurence chooses the largest of the tomatoes carefully, and then, his arm a wide arc, he smashes it against a telephone pole.

I watch red juice dripping against the splintered grey wood. The sun is dying. It paints the water tower shades of gold. The killdeers call to each other as they pass as silhouettes above the road. The crickets in the ditch speak to me of Omah's greenhouse where they hide behind earthenware pots.

What does Laurence know of hauling pails of water from the river, bending and trailing moisture, row upon row? What does he know of coaxing seedlings to grow or babies crying from dewdrops beneath the eye of God?

I turn from him and walk with my face reflecting the fired sky and my dust-coated bare feet raising puffs of anger in the fine warm silt.

"Hey, where are you going?" Laurence calls to my retreating back. "Wait a minute. What did I do?"

The fleeing birds fill the silence with their cries and the night breezes begin to swoop down onto our heads.

She sits across from me, Bible opened on the grey arborite, cleaning her wire-framed glasses with a tiny linen handkerchief that she has prettied with blue cross-stitch flowers. She places them back on her nose and continues to read while I dunk pastry in tea and suck noisily to keep from concentrating.

"And so," she concludes, "God called His people to be separated from the heathen."

I can see children from the window, three of them, scooting down the hill to the river and I try not to think of Laurence. I haven't been with him since the day on the road, but I've seen him. He is not alone anymore. He has friends now, kids who are strange to me. They are the same ones who make me feel stupid about the way I run at recess so that I can be pitcher when we play scrub. I envy the easy way they can laugh at everything.

"Well, if it isn't Sparky," he said, giving me a new name and I liked it. Then he also gave me a showy kiss for them to see and laugh. I pushed against his chest and smelled something sticky like jam, but faintly sour at the same time. He was wearing a new jacket and had hammered silver studs into the back of it that spelled his name out across his shoulders. Gone is the mousey step of my Laurence.

Omah closes the book. The sun reflects off her glasses into my eyes. "And so," she says, "it is very clear. When God calls us to be separate, we must respond. With adulthood comes a responsibility."

There is so much blood and death in what she says that I feel as though I am choking. I can smell sulphur from smoking mountains and dust rising from feet that circle a golden calf. With the teaching of these stories, changing from pleasant fairy tales of far away lands to this joyless search for meaning, her house has become a snare.

She pushes sugar cubes into my pocket. "You are a fine child," she says, "to visit your Omah. God will reward you in heaven."

The following Saturday, I walk a different way to her house, the way that brings me past the hotel, and I can see them as I pass by the window, pressed together all in one booth. They greet me as though they knew I would come. I squeeze in beside Laurence and listen with amazement to their fast-moving conversation. The jukebox swells with forbidden music. I can feel its beat in Laurence's thigh.

I laugh at things I don't understand and try not to think of my Omah who will have weak tea and sugar cookies set out on her white cloth. Her stained fingers will turn pages, contemplating what lesson to point out.

"I'm glad you're here," Laurence says, his lips speaking the old way to me. When he joins the conversation that leaps and jumps without direction from one person to another, his voice is changed. But he has taken my hand in his and covered it beneath the table. He laughs and spreads his plum breath across my face.

I can see Omah bending in the garden cutting flowers for weddings and funerals. I can see her rising to search the way I take and she will not find me there.

Inland by Carol Hoorn Fraser, 1970, oil on linen.

No Rinsed Blue Sky, No Red Flower Fences

DIONNE BRAND 1988

Ever since its first white settlers arrived in the seventeenth century, Canada has received immigrants, first from France and Britain, later from Central Europe and, more recently, from the Caribbean and Asia. For many, Canada has been their dream of a land of opportunity. Dionne Brand was born in the Caribbean and lives in Toronto as a poet and a writer of short stories. Here, she explores what happens when, for one Caribbean immigrant, the dream becomes a nightmare.

The apartment had tried to kill her again. She painted the walls as fast as she felt threatened. The city, she had been all through it in her searching, was dotted with bachelor apartments which she could not afford and hated anyway. As she moved from one to the other, she painted the walls. First, yellow, to be bright and then white to be alone. She told her friends that it was so that she could fill the rooms with her own self, so that she could breathe and put up her own paintings, her own landscapes on the walls. She had to live there but she didn't have to lose all sense of beauty, with their tatty walls and nothing in them as if no one ever lived there. Out of embarrassment she never said, but it was also because somehow she thought that the creditors, the mornings full of bills, would go away or she could feel them gone in the blinding white. Even with the walls so clean she never had money and when she didn't have it most, the apartment scared her.

It was an old building, four storeys (she hated high rises), wooden floors and old stucco walls. It creaked everytime someone passed in the corridors. When she had money the creaking sounded homely, like living with family. But when she was flat broke and depressed, the sound of footsteps outside the door made her jumpy. A queasy feeling appeared in her chest, as if a passage opened up between her throat and her heart and a fine and awful sound passed through, hurting the columns of arteries and the empty food cavity. The pain and the sound collapsed in her diaphragm. Her hand would reach to her soft stomach to assure the queasiness. But even her hands, as tender as they would have liked to have been, were frightened and upset the order of things, inciting her face and head to sadness and then reproach for such weakness and then pity for her blackness and her woman's body, and hopelessness at how foolish she was in not even being able to pay the rent, or fix her teeth, which she dreamt nightly fell out in her hands, bloodless.

Some mornings she woke up hearing the tree not far from her window sighing as an unexpected wind blew through it. Then she thought that she missed her children who were growing up far away without her. She wanted to gather up children and take them outside. They would like the sound, the island, the ferry. She could see their legs, bony and shine black, trembling to catch dirt and bruises.

The city could be so nasty when she had no money. Money was so important. If you had none, it made you feel as if you'd never done a thing in your life.

She'd worked "illegal" for six years. Taking care of children, holding their hands across busy streets, standing with them at corners which were incongruous to her colour, she herself incongruous to the little hands, held as if they were more precious than she, made of gold, and she just the black earth around. She was always uncomfortable under the passing gazes, muttering to herself that she knew, they didn't have to tell her that she was out of place here. But there was no other place to be right now. The little money fed her sometimes, fed her children back home, no matter the stark scene which she created on the corners of the street. She, black, silent and unsmiling; the child, white, tugging and laughing, or whining.

The city was claustrophobic. She felt land-locked. Particularly on humid days in the summer. She wanted to rush to the beach. But not the lake. It lay stagnant and saltless at the bottom of the city. She needed a piece of water which led out, the vast ocean, salty and burning on the eyes. The feel of the salt, blue and moving water, rushing past her ears and jostling her body, cleaning it, coming up a different person each time as she dove through a curling wave. Not knowing how it would turn out. A feeling of touching something quite big. She always imagined and tasted that plunge into the sea, that collision with the ocean. Suddenly every two years she felt like leaving, going to dive into the ocean just once. Scratch the money up, beg for it, borrow, work back-breaking weeks scrubbing floors; but leave.

Some mornings, she woke up looking up through the blind, the building, cloud, sky, surface. If the rain had fallen, rinsed blue, she hoped that the sea would be outside the apartment. Just there, just a few steps away. Some mornings she'd hear a small plane in the sky, a plane that would only fly over water, grass and red-wrung flower fences. The sea must be outside if all the sounds, plane, tree, 11 o'clock and rinsed blue sky were there. She lay on the floor loving the sound, making ready to see the sea a few steps from her window.

The threat of being evicted hung over her head. She thought that when she walked in the street, people noticed. They must've. If there was anything that tipped them off, it was the sign she wore in her eyes. She kept them lowered or at courageous times she stared until they removed their own eyes. On the bus, when she had the fare, she always stood, trying to appear thinner than she was, bent, staring out the window. She did not ask for apologies when people jostled her; she pretended that it did not happen. She did try sometimes. Sitting in two seats and ignoring people coming in but by the time two or three stops had passed she would ring the bell, get off the bus and walk quickly home.

Returning home her imagination tightened the walls of the apartment giving them a cavernous, gloomy look. She would lie on the floor and listen for footsteps in the corridor outside. The phone would ring and startle her. The sound would blast around in her chest and she would pray for it to stop, never thinking to answer it. It would course its way through her arms so that when she looked at her fingers they would seem odd, not hers or she, not theirs. Frightened until it stopped, then anxious at perhaps having missed a friend, listening to the ringing on the other side. Some of her friends knew that she never answered the phone and so would let it ring; but even though she knew the signal, she worried that perhaps other people, other than friends, had caught on. So when the ringing continued she was more afraid, thinking how persistent her enemies were.

The apartment had two rooms. She needed a place with two rooms. Each so that she could leave the other. The large room, when it was painted and when she threw out the bed seemed like someone else's place.

After she had sent the baby home, she had thrown the bed out. It was only a reminder of the long nine months and the hospital staff's cold eyes. When she'd left with the new baby she had pretended that someone was coming for her, waiting for her outside. But no one was there, no one knew and the name she had used was not hers. Nor did the baby exist. No papers. She would be found out if she registered the little girl. So small and wiry and no papers.

In the smaller room she kept a desk with a light to one corner. Two short black shelves were stuffed with books and papers which she could not throw out because she might need them as evidence that she tried to pay this bill or that one. She wrote anonymous letters to the immigration department asking if maybe she gave up would they still send her home . . . would they please have pity for her children.

A peacock rattan chair sat under the poster of home. A girl in a wet T-shirt, the sea in back, the sun on her body, represented home. Home had never been like that, but she kept the poster. Its glamour shielded her from the cold outside and the dry hills back home at the same time. The chair creaked everytime the humidity in the room changed.

In the days after she had read *Siddhartha*, someone had given it to her saying she would find peace, she lay for hours chanting "om." She attributed the creaking chair to the spirit of her great grandmother coming to visit. And for at least two months chanting "om" helped to calm her now chronic worrying. She sat cross-legged, her back vertical to the floor of her room, her hands, thumb and index finger softly clasped. So she buried the sound of the footsteps outside her door in long breathy "om," hoping that this one syllable expressed the universe. She actually saw the deep blue softing shape of "om," approached its glowing dark, telling herself that this would save her from the thin sharp voices on the phone, the girl in the wet T-shirt, the child with the white hand, the lewd traffic whirling in the middle of the street.

Once when she was nine, a long time ago, she'd seen a woman, old, bathing herself on the edge of the sand and water, dipping a cup, lifting it to her head, rubbing the shade of her long flaccid breasts. How bold, she thought, then walked past and turned slightly to see her again, still there, her face sucked to her bones, her eyes watery from age, unblinking. The woman, the gesture had stayed with her, marked her own breasts, her eyes. She willed herself not to feel hungry but to stay alive, present. She would lessen the number of her movements, she would design efficient strokes, nothing wasted. She would become the old woman. But how could she, so far from there.

There was a fireplace in the large room. Not a real one. One of those with two electric ranges strung across. It should have been real for its ornate facade. It may have been copper underneath the crude layers of paint. After two years of living in the apartment, she discovered that the fireplace worked. She found this out through the woman across the hall who invited her to a Christmas party. The woman was Jamaican, she had a fifteen year old daughter coming to meet her soon and a man friend who came every two weeks to sleep in the daytime on Sundays. He was tall, round, with a prickly thick moustache. The woman short, round, pulled her hair tightly back on these occasions. The rest of the time she wore it wild. All this she learnt by looking through the peep-hole at her neighbour when she was not afraid to look in the hallway.

Still, of all the places she had lived, she felt the strongest here. After years of dodging the authorities and the bill collectors, she had acquired some skill in putting them off. She realized that rudeness and sometimes a frank "I don't have any money," would do. She consoled herself that there was no debtors prison and often, when she could bring up the nerve, told them, "Take me to court." But creditors had more stamina than she and they would keep calling and threatening and she would break down and promise them her life. One had told her to go and sell her body if she had to and why were you people coming to this country, if you couldn't pay your bills, he had yelled into her ear. Her days then were heady. Each ring of the phone, each footstep in the hall, each knock on the door threatened to blow everything to hell. Those days the white walls came alive, glaring at her, watching her as she slept fitfully.

Mostly she did not remember her dreams. And mostly they were full of her watching herself as a guest at some occasion. She played all the parts in her dreams. Dreamer, dreamed. She was female and male, neutral. She never dreamed of anything that she was not. When she practiced to fly in her dreams, it was she who flew. Swooping down like a pelican into the water and changing course upward before touching. She had rehearsed that swooping since she was three, noticing the pelican's clumsy transforming glide into the sea at Point Fortin by the sea, its wet, full exit, its throat expanding fishlike. And she had practiced never reaching things too. One day a grove of orange balisier growing not far from the house caught her eye. After what seemed like hours of walking she never arrived at the grove and cried loudly until someone came to get her sitting in the dirt road.

Dreamer remained the same and often less than dreamed. It would surprise her to awaken to her thin, unvoluptuous body, limited to the corner of the floor on which she slept. Dreamed would return to limitlessness and the dreamer, to the acute clarity of the real—the orange juice, the telephone, the white Toronto street in winter.

Her sleeping was worse in the winter. There was an urgency to sleep at any hour. Especially when she had not seen the sun for days. A kind of pressure brought on by the grey sky, which she opened her eyes to on winter mornings, packed itself around her temples. It made her eyelids feel swollen and she spent half the day trying to recover herself. Each morning she would have to convince herself to get up from her half sleep which would make her sick. This half sleep did not belong to the dreamer or the dreamed. The avoided telephone calls recurred, answer no, ring no, answer, cupped to her mouth; the empty stomach; looking for a job, four hundred University eighth, no tenth floor, the immigration department, the smell of the lobby, it rose from the carpet, mixed with the air conditioner and the thud of the elevators. People hunched their shoulders, all the women, she included, perfumed to sickness, nylon encasing their legs, stood stiffly in the elevator ... pleading with someone there ... would they send her home, would they pity her children please ...

She fled. She could only perfect this flight in her dream. Rushing outside to the street, she plunged into the sea of snow, wrapped bodies, snorting cars making clouds of smoked ice. Reaching the subway, she rode to the end, where the work crowd thinned out—High Park, Runnymede, Old Mill. Coming up, the train reached a bare sky, scarred trees, gully, apartment building, stopping. She came out, let the train pass, sat looking through the glass of the station. She sat there for hours, getting back on the train, changing stations, only to find herself sometimes back in the elevator trying not to breathe the perfume, the smell of whiteness around her, a dull choking smell.

Wrestling to wake up, she tried to pull herself out of this half sleep which belonged to things out of her control. Movements rushed against each other. Shorter distances, more brusque, inhabited this sleep. Jumping to her feet, she realized that she was asleep. For the act of jumping found her lying, still on the floor, now surrounded by her body and her heavy face, with a film of flesh and thought to remove before rising and trying to decide what to do next.

The room becoming clearer than its uncharted corners. The tree over the next appartment building in the shadow of her thoughts, spread out its meagre twigs to form a shield against the cold, heavy air. Rushing to the window she looked at the street below, empty of people, still dark.

... this day if the sky could not move, if the heavy angle of the air would not shift to some other colour, at the corner she would knead a headache from her brow, walk to the middle of the street, the glowing centre of the wide lewd road and kneel down ...

Rushing to the window she looked at the street below, empty of people, still dark. Not sea and blue, no red flower fence and high sky.

Midday found her on the street corner, a little white hand in hers, her other hand kneading a headache from her brow.

Red Man Watching White Man Trying to Fix Hole in Sky by Lawrence Paul, 1990, acrylic on canvas.

The Serpent's Egg

GILBERT OSKABOOSE 1990

There was a time when "Canada" was known only to its original peoples, from the Haida on the Pacific to the Iglulik Inuit in the Far North, to the Beothuk in Newfoundland. Whether farmers or hunters, its many peoples shared a strong sense of living in fellowship with the land. Long before the coming of the French and British, the Ojibway people lived and prospered north of the Great Lakes. Here, an Ojibway writer uses a traditional story form to make some mocking comments on the benefits that Western "progress" in Canada has brought.

Long ago, when the world was young, a great Serpent came down from the north, and by its passing carved a mighty river through the Cambrian Shield in a land now called Northern Ontario.

Anishnawbek elders say it is so.

As she moved ponderously south the Serpent searched with a growing sense of urgency for she was ripe with new life and her time was near. In the wild barren lands between Elliot and Quirke Lakes she laid millions of tiny eggs, ominous little nodules that sank away from the light, deep into the bedrock, to lie dormant for millennia, waiting for their time to come.

And all around life went on. Her passing had created a river and the rains came and the river took on a life of its own. Schools of pickerel and bass swarmed through its cool depths; silver trout knifed through its brisk eddies, its warm shallows were patrolled by Giant Northern pike and shimmering dragonflies foraged up and down its length. On the glossy surface of the still backwaters black whirlyjig beetles spun in delirious circles. Otter and mink prowled its banks and in the air above, the tumbling flights of teal and mallard were the wind.

In time a wandering Ojibway scout found the sacred river and brought his people to live there in harmony with the land and its wild creatures. The men hunted bear and moose, the women gathered acorns, blueberries and the wild, sweet strawberries that grew in the meadows at the river's edge. Life was such that the children ran with wolves and the elders spoke with eagles.

In the time of the Moon of Popping Trees they sat around their fires and the elders told about the great Serpent. It was a good life, the way the Creator meant it to be. "But only the mountains live forever," it is said. For the First People change came in the form of The Others—a new race of humans that moved into the territory, strange people with pale faces, cold icy eyes and hair the colour of dry grass. The newcomers said they were trappers. In no time at all they had trapped all the beaver, otter and muskrats. They went away leaving the People with only trees and rocks.

A few years later they returned. This time they said they were loggers, and that was true because soon they had cut down all the big timber, the white pine and red pine and jackpine. Then they went away again, leaving the People with only the rocks. Everyone thought they had gone for good and the elders burned tobacco and thanked the Creator for small mercies.

But it wasn't meant to be. Somebody discovered a thing called uranium and The Others came back—this time for the rocks. They called themselves miners and they came armed with little black boxes that chattered like angry squirrels whenever they walked near the Serpent's nest. That made them happy and they started digging there, and didn't stop until they had found the Serpent's eggs.

The elders tried to warn them not to bother the eggs but the miners sent them away, and said they were old and foolish. They kept digging and wouldn't listen to anyone, not even their own medicine men who told them something was very wrong. The men were becoming ill. Their lungs blackened and they coughed up blood. But they kept digging and what they couldn't sell they threw into the river and the lakes. Then the river and the lakes died and still nobody paid any attention.

The miners ground the Serpent's eggs into a fine yellow powder they called "yellowcake" and sold it south of the medicine line to their brothers who were called "military tacticians" and "nuclear technicians." They cooked it up in big pots and made strong medicines from it. Many of them became sick and died after handling the yellowcake and the other medicines but nobody seemed to notice.

One of the medicines was called "radium" and they had their women paint it on dials that went into the cockpits of their tanks and airplanes so that their warriors could see to fight at night. The women put the tiny paint brushes into their mouths to wet and sharpen them into fine points, so that they could paint thin, neat lines. After a while the radium ate away their faces and those women died too.

Two sub-tribes known as the "peace-niks" and the "anti-nukes" became worried and tried to stop the military tribe but they were too small and weak. The military tribe was strong and had powerful allies who said that something called "acceptable loss factor" made it okay that a few people died from the medicines.

Another thing they made from the yellowcake was "nuclear bombs." They were long and slim and cold—just like the Serpent—and whenever they dropped one on another tribe that tribe disappeared in an instant, just as if the sun had fallen on it.

Two of them had been dropped on Japan. One of the bombs was called "Fat Boy" and Fat Boy must have been very heavy because when he landed on Japan 100,000 people died instantly. When the other tribes saw this they became frightened and asked The Others not to make any more but they wouldn't listen and kept on building "bigger and better bombs".

When they wouldn't stop other tribes figured they had better make some too, and pretty soon there was a big race to see which tribe could make the biggest and most. Very soon many of the tribes had bombs, enough to destroy the Earth 30 or 40 times over, even if a powerful medicine man could bring it back each time it was destroyed. In all of their recorded history The Others had never invented a weapon that—sooner or later—they didn't use on each other.

And so, that's the way the final war began. It started off with a lot of bad words that led to threats that ended up with them shooting their flying bombs at each other.

It wouldn't have been too bad if they just shot a few and then quit. Maybe their "acceptable loss factor" would have worked and only a few hundred thousand would have died, with a hundred thousand more dying later when the Serpent's breath settled to the ground. But it didn't work out that way, they just kept shooting more and more. One or two fires might have gone out by themselves or they could have been put out but ten thousand fires raged in an inferno that took on a life of its own. Giant firestorms never dreamed of created winds up to 1000 miles an hour. The event screamed and writhed and sucked whole cities and tribes into the Serpent's opening jaws. The Serpent had returned, lingered, and then gone—taking the entire Earth with it.

And in a galaxy far away a tiny green planet hung in deep space, in the gossamer web of another solar system, waiting for the white light from an incinerated planet as it sped across the dark chasm of a billion light years.

It was in the dead of winter when the light arrived and on the southern hemisphere of that tiny green planet peaceful people tending their flocks on rocky hillsides looked up, and a great shining light appeared in the eastern sky, and they were afraid, and stood in fear and awe, and wondered what this great sign could mean.

THE BEGINNING

Everyone Talked Loudly in Chinatown

ANNE JEW 1991

The so-called "generation gap" is often the subject of stories about clashes between adolescents, as they seek to become adults, and the adults who are closest to them, their parents. But what happens when members of a family have to cope with the additional complication of belonging to two cultures at once, the one that they were born in and the one they find in their new country? What happens when the ways of an ancient Eastern civilization clash with those of a modern Western culture such as urban Canada? The Chinese author, Anne Jew, leaves us with these dilemmas as three generations and two cultures are forced to meet one another.

Lately I have been walking home from school in the sunshine with Todd. It's October and the leaves have turned, though the temperature hasn't changed since the end of August. My father says the reason for this is there were two Junes in the Chinese calendar this year. I wonder if that makes this year thirteen months long or if one month is left out to fit into the regular calendar. But I don't ask. He would launch into a long, boring explanation of the history of the Chinese calendar and say it was superior to the Western calendar. If it was anyone else, I would probably ask.

Todd is very good looking. All the girls at school think so, and it makes me feel good when they turn to look at us walk down the hall together. Sometimes on our walk home we stop at the park to sit on the swings and talk. Actually Todd talks a lot and I listen. He usually describes his daily visit to the vice principal, the cars he wants, and the bands he likes. There is a Led Zeppelin logo drawn onto the back of his jean jacket in black felt pen which kind of bothers me.

"Have you ever really listened to their lyrics? They just make so much sense." It's his favourite band.

I try hard to stay interested in what he says and ask him questions, but mostly I end up nodding my head and saying, "Uh huh, uh huh." He doesn't seem to mind my quietness though. His eyes are clear blue, almost like glass, and it's hard to describe the feeling I get when he looks at me. My whole body feels like it's melting to the ground, and I'm always surprised to see that it hasn't.

Chinatown, Vancouver.

Today Todd walks me to the beginning of my block as usual and then crosses the street to go on. My mother would start to ask questions if she saw us together.

As I enter the house, I pass my grandmother's room to go upstairs. She is lying in there dying. I throw my bag into my room and head into the kitchen. I take out a bag of chips from the cupboard and pour a glass of orange juice and join my brother in the living room where he is watching a rerun of "The Brady Bunch." It's the one where Jan refuses to wear her glasses and smashes into the family portrait with her bike. After a while I forget about the Bradys and start to daydream about Todd.

The next thing I know, my mother is waking me up to feed my grandmother, whose hands shake all the time so she can't do it herself. My brother and I take turns every night.

I stand by the window in the kitchen waiting for my mother to put the food onto the dinner tray. I draw hearts encircling Todd's initials and mine on the steamed glass.

"Hey, what are you doing?" she asks. I quickly wipe away the evidence.

"Nothing."

Her dinner is basically the same every night—soup, rice with water, steamed vegetables, salted fish and a thermos of tea. When I go into the room, she is sleeping with the quilt drawn up to her chin, which is usually how I find her now. Before, my mother would move her to an armchair by the window where she could watch people walk by or she would watch the new television set my father bought for her. Her favourite shows were "The Roadrunner" and "The Beverly Hillbillies," both which I couldn't stand. She would point and laugh and mumble something in Chinese. She didn't understand them, but I think she liked their movements. Now she stays in bed, too weak to get up.

She looks really old. I think she's almost eighty-four, but no one knows for sure. They didn't have birth certificates in China then, and she had to lie about her age when she came over to Canada. Her skin is bunched up like fabric and it just kind of hangs from her cheekbones. But it feels thin and soft. I touched it once when she was asleep. Her hair is grey and white and oily. It's combed back, making her forehead look like a shiny grapefruit. The lobes of her ears have been stretched by the weight of gold earrings I have never seen her take off. She is hardly moving. She almost looks as if she were dead already.

"Grandmother, it's time to eat rice."

She briefly opens her eyes and then closes them again.

"Grandmother, it's time to eat rice," I repeat a little louder.

She opens her eyes again, and I bring the tray closer for her to see. She starts to sit up, and I put down the tray to help her. After I prop her up onto some pillows, I tuck a paper napkin into the neck of her pyjamas and begin to feed her. I really hate doing it and I always want it to be over as soon as possible. Luckily she has been eating less and less. I have been begging my mother to do it instead, but so far she hasn't given in.

"You're not the one who has to bathe her and change the sheets. Don't be so bad. You are the only one she has treated well. She is going to die soon anyway."

My mother can't wait for my grandmother to die. She is always telling my brother and me how she was treated like a slave by Grandmother when she first married my father.

"Why didn't you stand up for yourself?" I ask.

"Oh, you don't know what it was like then."

We start with the soup. The spoon makes a clanging noise as it knocks against her teeth, sending a shiver through me. She still has all of them, which is amazing since my mother already has false front teeth. She doesn't chew the food very much though. It stays in her mouth a while, and then she makes a great effort to swallow. I try to show her how to chew by making exaggerated movements with my mouth, but she just ignores me. She finishes the soup, and we start on the rice in water. Some of it dribbles out of her mouth, so I have to scrape it off her chin and spoon it back in like I'm feeding a baby. I feel disgusted and guilty and I don't know why. I also feel guilty for not spending more time with her and for not wanting to spend more time with her. Todd would die if he knew I had to do this.

She is a grown-up who has always taken care of me, but now I have to take care of her. It bothers me. She used to be different.

When I was little, she would take me to Chinatown every weekend. We would go to a small pastry shop at the corner of Pender and Gore. I would have a Coke and a coconut bun while she had tea with the owners. I had to call them Uncle and Auntie although they weren't related to us. They spoke to each other about the people they knew: who was dying, who was dead, whose daughter-in-law was lazy. They drew out their words into sighs and shook their heads at the misfortunes of others. Sometimes they would comment on me, looking at me as if I couldn't see or hear them.

"Look at that high nose. She doesn't look Chinese."

"She is such a shy cute girl."

I usually watched the customers, the bell tinkling above the door as they came and went. Most were short, chubby women with unmade faces and hair. They always looked tired and reminded me of my mother. They carried plastic shopping bags with different shop logos on them in Chinese characters, and their children would run around them as they tried to order. They would scream out their orders and at their children at the same time.

There were also old stooping men with brown spots on their faces and the odd gold front tooth, and old women with straight grey hair pinned back over their ears. The old people were always buried under layers of clothing no matter what season it was.

Each time we left, the owners would give me a box of barbecued pork buns to take home.

"Lin, thank Uncle and Auntie."

"Thank you Uncle and Auntie."

"What a cute girl."

My grandmother was very popular in Chinatown. While we shopped we would be stopped every few feet by her acquaintances. Everyone talked loudly and waved their arms. I couldn't understand why they had to be so loud. It seemed uncivilized. She also took me to visit her friends and I would occupy myself with extra game pieces while they played mah jong.

But as I started to grow up, I stopped going to Chinatown with her, where it was too loud, and then I stopped spending time with her altogether. I started to play with friends who weren't loud and who weren't Chinese. This upset my mother. She was suspicious of all other cultures. My best friend for a long time was a German girl who lived up the block. Everything was neat and orderly at her house, and her mother was a quiet, pleasant woman who offered me green apples from their tree. My mother only bought red ones in Chinatown.

Grandmother eats the rest of the rice and some vegetables and then motions me to stop. I wipe her mouth and chin and help her to lie down again. She closes her eyes, and I turn out the light and climb the stairs to my own dinner.

On our walk home from school the next day, Todd asks me to see a movie with him. I lie to my parents and tell them I am going with my girlfriend

Sandra. She swears not to say anything to anyone. Todd pays for the movie and the popcorn, and we sit in the back row of the theatre. He puts one arm around me, balances the bucket of popcorn on his knee, holds his drink between his legs, and eats and drinks with his other hand. I am impressed. I usually gorge myself on popcorn, but I feel compelled to eat one kernel at a time.

Halfway through *The Great Santini* and after we've finished the popcorn, Todd offers me a Certs. Then after a while he turns to me and kisses me on the lips. He opens his mouth on mine, and not knowing what to do, I open my mouth. I feel his tongue moving around in my mouth, so I move my tongue around in his. He still tastes faintly of popcorn under the flavour of the Certs. Just as I'm becoming used to the new sensation, he stops and kisses me on the lips and turns back to the movie. I can feel saliva clinging to the edges of my mouth, and not wanting to wipe it away with my hand, I press my face into his shoulder, hoping his shirt will absorb the moisture. It works.

As we leave the theatre, Todd takes hold of my hand. I am quickly beginning to fall in love.

"Now that was a great movie. That Robert Duvall guy is one harsh dude. What'd you think? Did you like it?"

"Yeah, I thought it was quite good."

"Yeah, it was great."

My hand feels good in his, but his strides are twice as long as mine, so our mismatched rhythms make us bounce along instead of walk. By now I am truly in love and I let him take me all the way home. Only the living room light is on, so we sit in the darkness of the carport in the back. Todd kisses me again and we move our tongues around. I am lost in the kissing until a car's headlights shine at us as it pulls into the driveway.

"Oh my God! It's my mother!"

I grab Todd's arm, and we run to the front of the house.

"Go! Hurry up!" He quickly kisses me and runs up the block. I stand around debating whether to go inside or escape to Sandra's house. I finally decide to go in. My mother and father are standing in the living room.

"How can you be so fearless! Going out with a white boy!" screams my mother.

My father walks up to me, his eyes wide with anger, and slaps me on the face. Automatically, I slap him back. He is stunned and I take the opportunity to run into my room. I expect him to come charging after me, but I am left alone for the rest of the night. It is only when the last light is turned out that I start to cry.

When I wake up hours later, my eyelashes are clumped together with dried tears. I didn't draw the curtains, so the moon shines into my room. Everything looks calm and quiet covered in moonlight. It comforts me. Todd, my father—it seemed to happen so long ago.

Only the hum of the fridge can be heard as I creep out into the hallway. I slowly climb down the stairs to my grandmother's bedroom. I imagine the sound of movement as I enter, but I stop and there is nothing. It is dark, so I feel my way over to the window and draw the curtains back a little. She is so still in the moonlight. I go to her and touch her face. It is soft, but cool. The shadows make it look almost ghostly. I take her hand, bony and fragile, and find she has no pulse. I drop it instantly and stand back to look at her. She is dead, I think. I stare at her face expecting it to move, but somehow it looks peaceful. I take her hand again, kneel beside the bed, and rest my head against her. Soon I am asleep.

Glossary

Arborite	a hard plastic cladding used for counters and table tops
bachelor apartment	a studio apartment or flat
bagboy	an adolescent or adult who packs a customer's goods at a grocery store
balisier	a West Indian plant with large leaves and bright orange flowers
bush	dense forest or wooded country
canned	dismissed from a job
Certs	a breath-freshening sweet
chips	potato crisps
corduroy	originally a French word for a type of cloth, here describing a road bed of small tree trunks, tightly packed cross-ways to the road's direction
corral	originally a Spanish word for a temporary protective circle of wagons, here used to denote a fenced enclosure for keeping animals
coulee	a French Canadian word for a deep ravine scooped out by heavy spring floods but dry in summer
curling sweater	a heavy wool sweater with a zip up the front
Door Prizes	lottery prizes, with the tickets bought before the event or at the door as one is entering
eight-pallet flat deck	an unarticulated lorry with a platform roughly thirty feet (ten metres) long
engineer	train driver
foxtail	a type of grass with soft, brush-like spikes of flowers
glad	the gladiolus flower
gopher	a common burrowing rodent on the prairies. The name comes from the French *gaufre*—a honeycomb
hackmatack	a type of larch tree. The name comes from the First Nation Algonquin people
hemlock	a conifer which grows up to 70 feet high, common in eastern Canada
killdeer	a bird found throughout Northern America. The early white settlers probably gave it this name, based on its call

mixer	a soft drink for mixing with alcohol, usually spirits
moccasins	soft leather footwear that is tied tightly around the calves. The name comes from the Algonquin people
muffin	a large, un-iced fairy cake
mukluks	high sealskin boots originally worn by the Inuit, from whose language, Inutituk, this word comes
Omah	the Russian word for grandmother
Opah	the Russian word for grandfather
packet	a boat carrying goods and mail regularly on a coastal run
parka	a hooded, wind-proof winter coat, mid-thigh in length. The word comes from the Inuit people of the western Arctic and means "outer skin"
pitcher	the equivalent in baseball of the bowler in cricket
prairie	the vast, rolling, grassy plains that cover most of western Canada. The word comes from the French Canadian for a meadow
rye	a whiskey distilled from rye
scrub	a made-up baseball game with fewer than the regulation number of players
Senior Matric	Matric is an abbreviation of the word Matriculation. Senior Matric refers to a set of examinations written in the final year of high school. Grades on these exams determined whether one would be admitted to a university
Shower	a women's gift party, for example "showering" gifts for an expected baby or for a bride-to-be
swale	a depression or hollow tract of land
swamper	a driver's assistant who helps to load and unload the lorry
tinderbox	before matches became the main means of getting fire, people used a tinderbox which contained a flint and steel for striking a spark, and tinder. Tinder was any substance (such as charred linen) which would catch the spark and which could then be gently blown into a flame
wolverine	a large animal of the weasel family, reputed to be vicious
yard	a back garden—originally from the Old English for an enclosure
yellow drop-slip	a memo to a lecturer indicating that a student has withdrawn from ("dropped out of") his or her class